The Mirror Caught The Sun

Operation Anthropoid 1942

John Martin

First Edition

A catalogue record for this title
is available from the British Library

ISBN 978 0 9561741 0 9

First Published MMIX

Published by John Martin Limited
www.heydrich1942.com

Dedicated to the memory of

Lorna Ellison

together with

Jan Kubis   and   **Josef Gabcik**

ACKNOWLEDGEMENTS

This book couldn't have appeared without the help of some great people, some of whom have asked to remain anonymous. Although I can't thank everyone who has helped me, there are people and organisations that I want to acknowledge, and these, in no particular order, are; Petr Adrian who finally got me inside Petschek Palace, Colonel J A Athill the British Defence Attache based in Prague who went above and beyond with his advice, help and patience in answering all my emails, the Hotel Duo in Prague and their driver Peter Smolick, Mike Janacek in Canada, Stanislav F. Brereton in Australia for his advice on the Gestapo investigation, historian Robert Ostland in Germany, Aneo Marinov at the Lidice Memorial, the Director of the Historical Archives in Prague Colonel Josef Zikes, Eva Pechova, Daniella White, Judith Runciman, Heider Heydrich for his hospitality and speaking about his father for the first time, my friend Nigel West, Czech Colonel Petr Miller, Slovak Colonel Micik, the Kubis family in particular Agata and Jirina Dusikova, Katarina Tomcikova from the Gabcik family, the immaculate 5th Special Forces Regiment in Zilina, my best friend Billy Midgley who accompanied me on trips especially to a freezing cold Fehmarn Island, Richard Beevers for his awesome contribution, Diana Hilson, Helena Vovsova, and the marvellous veteran organisations in both the Czech Republic and Slovakia.

However, special thanks are needed for the following:
Colonel Frantisek Veis without whom quite simply, this book would not and could not, have happened. Colonel Veis you are a credit to the badge you so proudly wear, and I only wish I was a soldier so I could rightly salute you.

Lorna Ellison for all the memories (and the laughs) she shared with me. I am so grateful, and so is the story of Operation Anthropoid.

Stanley Dallas who has always been there for me, and who came good again in the writing of this book. Stan you are the best!

My old history teacher John Phillips, who was an inspiration all those years ago, and who continued to be, in the writing of this book.

Peter and Colette Rogan for their constant pushing and reminding me of deadlines, and for all their help and patience in making some sense of my ideas.

Very special thanks though, must go to the great Neil Rees. Neil, who is an expert on the Czechoslovaks in the UK, was always only an email away, not only as a constant source of expert advice, but as a true friend. Thank you Neil, though that seems so inadequate for all that you unselfishly gave to the writing of this book.

Finally, thank you to Joanne for all the encouragement, love and patience while I have been writing this book. (I promise I will finally tidy my office now!)

Foreword

In Britain Winston Churchill set up the Special Operations Executive (SOE) to set Europe ablaze. Different Allies had their own sections and planned operations for their occupied homelands. British planes dropped parachutists into different countries. To get to Czechoslovakia British SOE flights had to overfly the Third Reich making it a hazardous journey, let alone the dangers of any operation. Yet they planned one of the most notorious operations of the whole war, the plan to kill Reinhard Heydrich. Following the operation, the retributions were horrendous.

John Martin has been fascinated by this subject for many years and has spent an incredible amount of time researching it. With great enthusiasm, he tells the story in his own way, and takes you on the trail of Reinhard Heydrich and his Czechoslovak assassins. I came across John Martin whilst researching the Czechoslovak Government in Exile. The Czech Embassy told me about him. Since then, we have been in touch almost on a daily basis. John Martin has gone into the subject in immense length. There are already a number of books on this subject, but none with the concern for the tiniest detail that John Martin brings.

Neil Rees

Author of "The Czech Connection – The Czechoslovak Government in Exile in London and Buckinghamshire during the Second World War"

Preface

I've been asked so many times how a professional comedian gets an interest such as the subject of this book? Let me explain as best as I can.

I have been a professional comedian since 1983. It's the job I always wanted since I was a young boy growing up in Liverpool. Since I was that same young boy, I grew up enthralled at the stories my father told me about his time in the army. He joined the British Army during the Second World War. He was put in the 79th Armoured Division, which was a specialised tank unit, formed for the D Day landings of 1944. My father was there, actually there at D Day.

Ever since I was old enough to realise it, he became my hero.

This led to me developing a passion for battle stories and all those brave enough to serve. I devoured every book on wars throughout the ages and still do today. Eventually, a story just touches your heart and this is exactly what happened to me the first time I read about Operation Anthropoid. I read wide-eyed a magazine article and I just had to know more about it and visit the places concerned.

Operation Anthropoid took place in what was then German-occupied Czechoslovakia. It was the attempt by a small number of patriots to rid both Czechoslovakia, and the world, of one of Hitler's top henchmen, Reinhard Heydrich.

It came at a very high price but this doesn't reduce the bravery of the men and women who helped make it successful. Heydrich was reducing the people in the Czech lands to gross unfairness. The people had very little choice but to acquiesce to the demands made on them, to work flat out in the armaments factories and to toe the line. The people often referred to him as the *blonde beast* but for the Nazis he was producing great results and was one of its brightest stars. Something had to be done to show the world that the Czechoslovak people could fight back..

I am, in no way, claiming that my book can ever do justice to the people who were involved. What I offer is passion for the subject. All I am trying to do, all I ever try to do with the many lectures I give on the subject, is to highlight what these people went through, and what they achieved in the face of terrible odds. If their memories live on for one extra day because of my book, then it will all have been worthwhile.

Finding information about Anthropoid has not always been easy-going though. To all those "official" people who were dismissive or who told me to forget it, and we have moved on, I say fine, its right to move on, and progress is correct. But please, don't forget the people who gave everything so that the world could move on. I can certainly understand the reluctance of some people in authority, particularly in the Czech Republic, in wanting to keep Operation Anthropoid locked away. Some officials are perhaps ever mindful of what it cost in terms of human lives. Thousands died in the Czech lands because of it and it's still debated there whether the price paid was too high.

Many doors were closed and stayed closed to me during the course of my research, and many requests for information went unanswered, which is a lot more frustrating than a negative response. Maybe I don't understand the politics of it all, but all I ever I wanted to do was to pay tribute to the brave people who suffered so much under the Nazi jackboot. Strangely though, I have had more co-operation from the Heydrich family than from some official sources in the Czech Republic.

My journey to try to find the truth about Anthropoid, though a labour of love, has been long and, at times, strange. It's taken me all around Britain, to many parts of the Czech Republic, various places in Germany, and to an airport in Slovakia with what must have the world's smallest luggage trolleys! I've been propositioned in Berlin, been offered the honour of killing a pig in the Czech Republic, been freezing in January in northern Germany and boiling hot in the middle of a Czech summer, and have been fully initiated in the culture of drinking the potent Slivovice drink (made from apricots or plums), so beloved by many Czechs and Slovaks! I spent two great days with the Special Forces Regiment in Zilina now named after one of the soldiers of Anthropoid, and to them I am indebted. They are a credit to the name. I have walked many cemeteries, including every single inch of the Invaliden cemetery in Berlin (twice). I scoured archives in the UK (the UK file on Anthropoid was released in March 1995). Finding Lorna Ellison was a major breakthrough for me. I was able to take her to visit the places associated with her *dear Czech friends*. With great sadness for me, Lorna passed away before the publication of my book and is greatly missed. I found Heydrich's son and daughter, and his gardener. Heider Heydrich who was 8 at the time of his father's death, gave me the first interview he has ever given on the subject of his father. Heider turned out to be a most pleasant man, and I am so indebted to him not just for agreeing to speak to me, and for his hospitality, but for all the information he gave me about his father's early life, and the subsequent years after Anthropoid. Reinhard Heydrich to his family was just "Papa", and the fact that he was a human-being brings home the whole futility of the years that he was one of the most feared men in the world.

Reinhard Heydrich cannot be defended, and even if he could, why would you want to? But at the war's end there was a definite tendency to blame him for many things that he couldn't have been responsible for. Clearly working on the assumption that a dead man couldn't answer back, top Nazi's blamed Heydrich for many things to take the heat off themselves. Indeed, a secret report from an alleged Soviet source at the time stated that Heydrich was finally killed by the Nazi's to *"deliberately and suddenly accentuate Nazi oppression on the Czechs"*. Whilst new evidence shows this was not the case, it is undeniable that many of the atrocities happened as retribution for Heydrich's death, not as a result of a decision made by him. I truly believe that the attack on Heydrich frightened the top brass of the Nazis and that they came down hard afterwards in an attempt to try to dissuade people from future attacks. Indeed, only a couple of days after the attack on Heydrich, the head of the Czech Secret Intelligence in London, Colonel Frantisek Moravec sent a Most Secret and Personal report to UK authorities, where he stated that *"....I hope the splendid example of Anthropoid will shortly be followed in other parts of the world."* Clearly this thinking was around at the time.

But it wasn't just at the end of the war that Heydrich was blamed. I read a book recently where it said *" .... Reinhard Heydrich summoned the Jews to the gas chambers in November 1943."* Heydrich died on 4th June 1942, so this could not be true.

I've met and been welcomed by the families of some of the men involved in the Anthropoid operation itself, and other people from that time. Some of their stories have reduced me to tears, and yet they are so proud telling them. I even found a couple who now have in their possession the actual uniform Heydrich was wearing at the time of the attack. It has never been washed.

I have included some initials in the book, which are the standard abbreviated titles of the organisations involved. But briefly they are:

The SS- its full name was the Schutzstaffel. This was a Nazi elite organisation, which originally was intended to be Adolf Hitler's personal bodyguard. All its members swore an Oath of Loyalty to Hitler. This organisation grew to be a large select group with nearly 1 million members, and was almost a separate army for the Nazis, different from the official German army.

The SD- inside the SS was an intelligence unit run by Heydrich. Its full title was the Sicherheitsdienst, and became known by the initials SD. Heydrich was wearing an SD patch stitched on his sleeve on the day he was attacked.

RHSA- The Reichssicherheitshauptamt, or Reich Security Head Office. This incorporated the police forces of the Third Reich, all under one banner once the war began, and overall was run by Heydrich.

The Gestapo- full title Geheime Staatspolizei, which was the Secret Nazi State Police.

The SA- started out as basically thugs who defended Hitler at his rallies, and who went to meetings of other parties such as the Communist party, and heckled and disrupted the speakers. They created scenes of violence wherever they went.

My journey to discover more about Operation Anthropoid has been long, exciting, emotional, and frustrating, full of highs and lows, but it's been a journey, quite honestly, that I wouldn't have missed for the world.

Reinhard Tristan Eugen Heydrich

Heydrich

Heydrich: The best man in the SS, and a pillar of the New Order. The mere mention of his name was guaranteed to terrify the bravest of men. Whole nations would shake with fear and trepidation at the forecast of his arrival. A man with the power of life and death over millions of people.

Heydrich: Many called him The Hangman of Prague, some The Butcher of Prague. Adolf Hitler, his boss, once described him as *"the man with a heart of iron"*

Heydrich: A genocidal fanatic; a rabid anti-Semite; a desk-based mass murderer; a sexual deviant; a gatherer of secrets; an ace blackmailer and schemer; a man up to his elbows in the blood of the Third Reich.

Heydrich: A split personality; a man with few, if any, moral scruples; a man who was more than willing to use any method or means to further his aims; a sinister genius; vain.

Heydrich: Described by Nazi spy chief Walter Schellenberg as *"the hidden pivot around which the Nazi regime revolved, and the puppet master of the Reich."*

Heydrich: A possible future successor to Hitler

All the above are words I've read to describe Reinhard Heydrich. Because many people have asked me "Who was Heydrich?" here is a brief outline of his life and career.

Reinhard Tristan Eugen Heydrich first entered the world at 10.30am on Monday 7th March 1904. He was born in the German town of Halle an der Salle, near Leipzig in the Saxony Kingdom of the German Empire.

Reinhard was the second of three children. His sister Maria was born in 1901 and his younger brother Heinz in 1906. All three children were the result of a strict Catholic marriage between Bruno Heydrich and Elizabeth Krantz. From many accounts, much favouritism was shown to the daughter Maria, which could possibly have led to future psychological problems for Reinhard.

Bruno Heydrich was an accomplished musician, who had started his own prosperous music academy in Halle. Elizabeth Heydrich brought the children up as staunch supporters of the Roman Catholic faith and discipline was strict within the family home.

Unfortunately for young "Reini", as the family called him, he had a high pitched, almost feminine, voice and this led to him often bearing the brunt of his class friends' taunts. Even more disturbing for a young boy growing up in early twentieth century Germany was the fact that the family were often taken to be Jewish. It's thought that this rumour emanated from his grandmother's second marriage and it was a rumour that was to follow Reinhard throughout his life and career in the SS. No evidence to substantiate this ancestry rumour has ever been produced. Maybe that could be more sinisterly rewritten as *"no evidence has ever been disclosed."* But whatever the case, it was always a long shadow to the Heydrich family. Some reports even have it that Hitler was aware that Heydrich had this Jewish connection but kept it as a way of blackmailing him should the need ever arise. The "connection" is thought to have come about as a result of Heydrich's grandmother Ernestine marrying for a second time, to a man, some sixteen years younger by the name of Gustav Suss, a name that was considered Jewish at the time. In fact, the man in question was not Jewish. Also, it is written that in his father's musical act, Bruno performed what is called an "Isidor" which is a caricature of a Jewish man, leading to taunts by school friends and shouts of *"here comes Issy Heydrich"*. Anyway, by then, Reinhard Heydrich had been born and was free in the bloodline, but he inevitably inherited the problem.

Being a teenager at the end of the First World War had a formative effect on Reinhard Heydrich. As poverty and soaring inflation rocked the German economy causing social chaos, Reinhard became aware, at an early age, of political strife. Like many people of his generation, the young Heydrich was smarting and felt betrayed at the humiliation of his beloved country following its defeat in World War One. Massive reparations, loss of German land under the Versailles Treaty and economic collapse due to the Great Depression, meant that this once-proud nation was stripped of its power. This belittlement led to anger, resentment and much discord.

On 30th March 1922, Reinhard Heydrich joined the German navy. Unfortunately for him his physical appearance, described as tall, blonde with feminine hips, added to his woes. His fingers had been described as *long like the legs of a spider* and all this, together with his high pitched voice, meant that the childhood taunts continued. Only his outstanding musical prowess with the violin endeared him to his fellow sailors.

Being a keen young man in the navy led to him discovering a naval hero, a man by the name of Wilhelm Canaris. Canaris was to become one of Heydrich's few close friends and even closer neighbour in later life when they both lived in the Sudende, (or South end) suburb of Berlin. Canaris was also to become a close colleague when he became head of the Abwehr, the German Military Intelligence.

Heydrich quickly rose up the ranks in the navy and used any free time he had to become a very accomplished fencer, horse rider and swimmer. He was ranked amongst the top ten for the whole of European fencing competitions, although he never took defeat lightly! It is said that any defeat would lead to him blaming the referee. In his book"Heydrich. The Pursuit of Total Power" Deschner described an incident when Heydrich failed to win a particular fencing match. He stated *"Heydrich flung his sword to the ground in disgust."* (According to Heydrich's own family, when I spoke to them, the only thing he hated more than losing was when an opponent made no effort to beat him out of fear or deference to his title!)

In November 1930, Reinhard met Lina von Osten from the Baltic island of Fehmarn, the woman with whom he was to share the rest of his life. Almost on the first date Heydrich proposed marriage. Lina was taken aback but she soon agreed and the young couple were engaged the following month. Unfortunately for the loving couple, it transpired that Heydrich had possibly made a similar proposal to another young lady. There are various accounts of this, ranging from him making the girl pregnant, to sexual dalliances, but whatever the truth of the matter, Reinhard chose Lina. However, it seemed that the other young lady's father had some influence, as he was reputedly an important businessman with influential friends. He complained officially to the naval authorities about Heydrich and an enquiry was initiated. Though the young Reinhard was confident of a victory in the hearing, and continued to cast doubt on the girl's story, Heydrich was found guilty of "behaviour unbecoming an officer and a gentleman" and was dismissed from the navy. Heydrich now found himself about to be married and unemployed.

Contrary to opinion, it was not Lina who introduced Reinhard to the SS. It was, in fact, his mother Elizabeth who got young Reinhard a meeting with the then little-known SS leader Heinrich Himmler, through a well-placed family friend called Karl von Eberstein. At the time the SS was a small and insignificant organisation but it did possibly offer prospects for an unemployed military man. At the meeting Himmler (who was unwell at the time and tried to cancel Heydrich's appointment) was immediately struck by Heydrich's Nordic appearance. He asked Heydrich to write him a short essay on how he would organise an Intelligence Service. Heydrich, drawing on experience gleaned from reading cheap spy thriller books, spent less than thirty minutes on the assignment and Himmler was impressed enough to offer him a job, there and then. The new recruit was given SS number 10120. Now employed again, the delayed wedding could go ahead and the happy couple were married on 26th December 1931 near Fehmarn Island.

Now a married man, Heydrich turned his attentions to his new-found work. He laboured with zest and gusto implementing a central card filing system on known criminals and suspects. He also worked hard at recruiting the right people to work with him in the Intelligence Service, otherwise known as the SD. He helped establish total social control over the civilian population.

Following Hitler's appointment as Chancellor of Germany, Heydrich set about completely reorganising the policing system with himself as its head. In 1936 Heydrich was also given the prestige appointment of overseeing the Berlin Olympic Games, which would seem a perfect appointment with him being a talented and keen sportsman.

In 1939 the whole policing system was reorganised under one banner. The Gestapo, the criminal police and the SD were all combined to form the Office of Reich Security, or RHSA. Reinhard Heydrich was its top man.

Heydrich meanwhile had also been busy usurping the power of the SA, which was under the leadership of Ernst Rohm. In what became known as "Night of the Long Knives", the leadership of the SA were either imprisoned or murdered by Heydrich's henchmen. The SA was largely made up of uncompromising thugs who roamed the streets on the lookout for violence and had been in competition with the SS for some of the security matters in the Third Reich. Heydrich had now been influential in cutting it off at its head. This eliminated all meaningful opposition within the German borders.

Heydrich had also been very influential in the infamous "Kristallnacht", or "night of the broken glass", where many Jewish shops and businesses had been attacked and looted in Germany on the night of 9th November 1938. This was, in reality, the first State-directed riots against the Jewish population. Hundreds lost their lives. About thirty thousand were sent to concentration camps. Tens of thousands of Jewish businesses and about a thousand synagogues were destroyed. The name Kristallnacht comes from the shards of broken window glass that were said to be evident all over Germany.

Heydrich was heavily involved in the operation that led to the start of World War 2, when he helped direct the false attack on a German radio station just inside Poland that gave Germany a so-called excuse to invade Poland. This became known as the Gleiwitz Incident, because it happened in the small town of Gleiwitz. The truth of the matter though was that the attack had been planned involving Heydrich's office and, in fact, the Polish "fighters" who attacked the radio station were concentration camp victims dressed up in Polish uniforms. Germany invaded Poland the next day under the guise of retaliation.

Heydrich was instrumental in organising and issuing orders to what were called Einzatzgruppen. These were units of about 1000 men, mainly SS people, who followed the German army in to battle, mostly on the Eastern front, and set about murdering large-scale groups of the local population such as Jewish people, Gypsies, Communists and anyone considered in any way undesirable to the Third Reich. These Einzatzgruppen were in 4 different groups (A, B, C, and D) and were assigned their own geographical area of responsibility. They were responsible for many of the atrocities committed outside of the concentration camps. It is estimated that over 1 million men, women and children were murdered at the bloody hands of these Einzatzgruppen killing squads. Most of the killings were meticulously recorded and listed in official journals.

It would seem that there was no end to Heydrich's murderous trickery and duplicity and his influence was most definitely on the rise. Whatever the problem, Heydrich seemed to be at the centre of the maelstrom. Promotion followed promotion and his control of Germany's security forces continued to grow. He also became head of the International Police Congress, the forerunner of Interpol in 1938.

In January 1942 Heydrich's infamy took on a whole new spectrum when he organised and chaired the meeting at the villa in Wannsee in Berlin that decided the "Final Solution" to the Jewish problem. This ultimately led to the murder of millions of people. Though Heydrich often complained in private that his job meant he was the dustbin man for the Reich, he certainly set about his task with energy, determination, and organisation. In the 1961 trial of Adolf Eichmann, (who was notorious for his part in the ill-treatment of Jewish people and who supposedly took the notes in the Wannsee meeting) Heydrich was cited as being pivotal to Eichmann's defence in the following statement made to the court: *"Wannsee gave Heydrich the authority to regard himself as having authority in all Jewish matters."*

Munich

With the rise of Hitler's Third Reich, Europe was under immense threat. In order to try to stop the Nazi's ambitions and buy the Allies some time, the British Prime Minister, Neville Chamberlain, made a number of urgent visits to Hitler's headquarters. Eventually a deal, involving Hitler and Chamberlain, coupled with the leaders of France and Italy, was reached in the early hours of 30th September 1938. The infamous Munich Agreement document was signed, leading to what Chamberlain described as *"peace in our time"*.

This so-called Munich Agreement, which decided the immediate fate of parts of Czechoslovakia, was drawn up without any Czechoslovakian representation. Indeed, the Munich Agreement is known today in the Czech Republic as the "Munich Dictate" and much resentment is still felt by Czechs, at an arrangement that largely used their country and new found independence as a pawn or bargaining tool. However, I have always felt some sympathy for Chamberlain. I believe he had a desire for peace for Europe, albeit a naive one. Some even argue that Chamberlain knew exactly what he was doing and that, in fact, what he was doing was buying some time for Britain and France to build their armies up.

Britain and France hoped that the agreement would satisfy Hitler but history has shown that was clearly not to be the case. Hitler probably couldn't believe his luck at the ease in which his demands were met and, far from satisfying him, the agreement only served to whet his appetite. World War 2 broke out twelve months later.

In 1938 Hitler had ordered his troops into Czechoslovakia, or at least the parts that excluded Slovakia. At first they only went into the disputed border areas of the Sudetenland. Soon afterwards they occupied the rest of the Czech lands. Slovakia signed a peace treaty with Germany and, in the words of Adolf Hitler, *"Czechoslovakia has now ceased to exist."*

On March 16th 1939, Hitler issued a decree establishing the Protectorate of Bohemia and Moravia, which made up the majority of the Czech lands. A "Protectorate" was the title used to describe a country that had been taken over by Germany, had become dependant on Germany and was now to be fully incorporated into Germany's Third Reich Empire. Therefore, the term Reich Protector was used to describe the person in charge of "protecting" Germany's interests in the occupied territories. All military and economic responsibility in the Protectorate fell under the jurisdiction of the Reich Protector. The Czech lands were then divided in to 2 areas, Bohemia and Moravia. At first the Nazis were planning on having two almost separate States but then decided on it all being under the one office. The Czechs living in these areas were often referred to as "Protectorate Nationals". Meanwhile, Hitler visited Prague, and right behind him, everywhere he went, was Reinhard Heydrich.

A couple of days later, on March 18th 1939 Hitler appointed an old army Diplomat called Konstantin von Neurath to the newly-created position of Reich Protector of Bohemia and Moravia. The Nazi occupation would seem to be complete.

Almost immediately laws were established, decreeing that the "Protectorate", was fully incorporated in to Hitler's Third Reich.

In Prague, German became the official language, public transport had to display the stops in both the Czech and German language (which was hated by the local population) and even driving on the left was replaced by driving on the right.

Total subservience was the order of the day and the Gestapo moved in to break up any form of resistance. Czechoslovakia was very rich in natural and human resources and this is what the Nazis needed for its war effort, with the Second World War breaking out on 3rd September 1939.

Huge factories, such as the Skoda works in Plzen, were turned over to produce armaments and 100% production was required. This massive Skoda factory was said to employ up to 35,000 people during the Occupation, including people who were making guns, shells and even undercarriages for German aeroplanes.

However, by September 1941, Czech resistance to the occupiers was becoming much more evident. Press cuttings from the time were of train derailments, lost production and boycotts. Strikes and sabotage threatened the transport system, and Prague was a vital railway link to the Eastern Front. Open demonstrations such as the removal of German street signs were prevalent. A thriving black market economy developed alongside boycotts of the German-produced newspapers. Probably though, the most important feature of growing resistance was slow-downs in the munitions factories which threatened the very fabric of the occupation. The Czech Resistance movement was known to be in frequent radio contact with London. (Many of these radio messages from London urged the people to *work slowly* in the factories, with some reports saying that production in the armaments factories fell by as much as 25-30%) Clearly something had to give with the German masters. On the 27th September 1941, von Neurath was replaced, on the pretext of illness, by that much more fearsome man, SS Obergruppenfuhrer Reinhard Heydrich. (Heydrich had been promoted to Obergruppenfuhrer on the same day.)

The new Acting Reich Protector

Prior to all this, the Czechoslovak army had tried to defend its homeland when the Germans first threatened. Their obsolete weapons were absolutely no match for the newly equipped modern German army and reluctantly they were ordered to give the Germans a free rein. Some of the Czechoslovak soldiers managed to escape firstly to Poland and then on to France where they helped in that country's fight as members of the Foreign Legion. Some eventually made their way to Britain, many sailing in to Liverpool, all with the hope of reorganising and fighting another day. One of these escaping soldiers was Jan Ludvig Hoch who changed his name and became a famous newspaper publisher after the war. He was Robert Maxwell. (Maxwell was expelled from this Czechoslovak army at Cholmondeley on 27th July 1940 for activity including rebelling against Benes, the Czech leader in exile. He was then put in to the British Army Pioneer Corps.)

Czechoslovak pilots were incorporated into the RAF and many of them took part in the Battle of Britain, as well as many other missions. Czechoslovak soldiers were also prominent in the defence of Liverpool from attack by the Luftwaffe. The main bulk of the Czechoslovak army was finally pulled together and stationed in the grounds of Cholmondeley Castle near Whitchurch, in North West England.

The Czechoslovak President, Edvard Benes, and his military intelligence team led by Colonel Frantisek Moravec, had also made their way to Britain where they eventually set-up what was finally recognised as a Government-in Exile.

President Edvard Benes

At Cholmondeley Castle, the Czechoslovak army, although largely living in tents, started to become properly organised, retrained, and re-equipped. Some of these displaced soldiers had been awarded medals for their bravery against the enemy, especially in France. That was the case of two close friends, Josef Gabcik and Jan Kubis. Both men were presented with the Czechoslovak War Cross by President Benes and both men were awarded medals for bravery in France. (When Josef was leaving for Poland to escape the Nazis, he said to his sister-in-law Maria *"Today you are cleaning my shirt for the last time. I will come back in 10 years"*)

The Czechoslovak Brigade stationed near Whitchurch, proved popular with the local population. The locals did what they could to befriend the Czechoslovak soldiers. Josef Gabcik and Jan Kubis were befriended by a family who lived in a small village three miles outside of Whitchurch, a village called Ightfield. This family was called the Ellison family.

Lorna's Story

In the story of Operation Anthropoid the Ellison family feature very prominently in the lives of Jan Kubis and Josef Gabcik. This typical English family, with a son in the RAF and two teenage girls living at home, befriended the two soldiers and made them welcome within their family home. The Ellison family didn't have an abundance to eat with the war rationing being in place but all they had they shared with two soldiers who had found themselves many miles from home.

Mr and Mrs Ellison had sadly passed away, as had the eldest daughter Edna, when I eventually found Lorna, the younger of the two teenage daughters. I had to work hard to track Lorna down. My search started at the church in Ightfield after having been told that the locals knew about them but it was thought they had passed away. I searched the local cemetery for a grave to give me clues. By chance I bumped in to a local man who, when he found out what I was doing, directed me to a house in the village. The people who lived in this house knew of the Ellison family and said that they thought a member of the family worked in a local garage. I learned that the female member of the family had left the employment of the garage but the proprietor thought she had gone to work in a local supermarket. Again, I was too late as she had left that job. At each place I visited I left my contact details. Imagine my delight, when, only a couple of days later, I got a phone call from a lady called Diana Hilson, who it turned out, was the eldest daughter of Lorna Ellison. She had heard that I had been trying to find her mother and when she revealed that her Mum was alive and well, I could have jumped for joy! I immediately made arrangements to travel and see Lorna Ellison, who was now living on the outskirts of London.

Our meeting to discuss events that happened over 60 years ago, was an emotional moment for Lorna. Even though I had made an appointment to travel to her home and so not completely unknown to her, I was still a stranger turning up and asking her questions about a part of her life that had happened so long ago. We were about to tap in to memories that Lorna had kept largely to herself for all those years. Lorna was married after the war and had raised a family but she was now sadly widowed. She was now ready to share with me all that she had bottled up for so many years. This turned out to be a major breakthrough in my research and, quite honestly, in the research of Operation Anthropoid. In virtually all accounts of the men involved, there had been a gap in the knowledge that only someone like Lorna Ellison, with her memories, could fill.

I tried not to badger Lorna with question after question but rather listened to what she had to say. I did want to start with knowing how the Ellison family first came in to contact with Jan Kubis and Josef Gabcik. Lorna now takes up the story:

"My elder sister Edna and I had been to the cinema in Whitchurch. In those days, especially with the war being on, there wasn't much else to do. As we walked to get our bus home, we passed a soldier in uniform, sitting on a wall near the car park. He was also waiting for a bus, to take him back to Cholomondeley Castle. He smiled as we went past, and when we got on the bus, he came up, wrote something on a piece of paper, and passed it to us through the bus window.

My sister Edna opened the note and said "Ooh look, he wants to meet us here tomorrow afternoon. What do you think Mum will say?" When we got home and showed mum the note, Mum said 'I don't mind, behave yourselves and go on the condition that you are both back here by 5pm.'

The teenage Lorna

The next day was a Sunday. There were no buses, so Edna and I cycled the 4 miles in to Whitchurch and Jan was there sitting on the same wall. We went and sat by him and we started chatting. We asked him all about himself, where he was from and where he had been. I remember there was a little café across the road that sold tea, so we all went there. Contrary to what some books about the men said later, Jan spoke good English.

Jan said to us 'Do you come to town often?' and we explained that we came to Whitchurch to go to the cinema or do some shopping. Jan then said 'This time next Saturday, you meet me here?'

We went again the following Saturday and this time Mum came with us. She met Jan and Jan was a gentleman, a perfect gentleman. We all went to the cinema, and afterwards Jan walked us to our bus and said 'Same time next week?' Jan was such a polite man, always making sure that he walked on the outside of us and helping us up the steps of the bus.

The following week we all went to the cinema again and afterwards, when we were walking to the bus, Mum said to Jan, 'How long do you wait for your bus?', and Jan said 'One or two hours maybe'. So Mum said 'Well, you would have time to come home with us, to see where we live and have a cup of tea. You would be made welcome'. So Jan Kubis came home with us that night. As we got off the bus near our house, a strange thing happened. There were two white gates that opened up in to our garden, and on reaching this Jan suddenly stopped, looked around and said 'It's just like home' and he almost cried. He said it reminded him of his home in Czechoslovakia.

That evening Jan met Dad and they both had a long chat about the war and also about the First World War. We all got on so well, that every Saturday we met Jan and took him home with us for tea and a snack. After a number of weeks of this, Mum said to Jan 'Would you like to bring a friend that you could speak to in your own language?' Jan always had his camera and photograph album with him, so this day he put the album on the table and said to Edna and I 'You choose one'. We all had a look through it having a good old giggle and eventually we stopped on one picture and said 'That one', because the man in the photograph had a right old mischievous grin. Jan couldn't believe it and said, 'How strange, that's my best friend Josef'. It was a photograph of the two men taken together whilst they were fighting in Africa. I remember the photograph well, as they were both sat on a wall. So the next visit he brought Josef with him and that was the beginning of our very special friendship."

Lorna went on to explain all about this very special friendship with Jan and Josef, so special that the men were even allocated their own bedroom in the modest house. "They always slept in what we called the blue room, simply because it was painted blue. Whenever they were on leave or at weekends, the men would come to stay. They were always in uniform and always perfect gentlemen. Jan was the quieter of the two and Josef was always full of fun and mischief, always telling jokes and making us laugh. He was just like a cheeky schoolboy much of the time, hardly ever serious. He was always the joker and gave us a number of nicknames, with one I remember as Co-Co. Why he called me that I don't know but that was typical of the Josef I knew. I even smile to myself these days when I think of him, he was so full of life."

Often the girls went for walks with the 2 soldiers or, on other occasions, Jan and Josef would borrow bicycles from Lorna's parents, so they could all go for bike rides out in to the country.

The friendship lasted over 12 months. Lorna said that both Jan and Josef spoke good English, and when Gordon Ellison (Lorna's brother) was visiting, on leave from the RAF, Jan Kubis often spoke to him in German as both Jan and Gordon spoke the language well. Gordon and the two soldiers also became close friends. Gordon was to tell Lorna later that Jan had shown him scars on his rear that fascists had done to him, in the shape of swastikas.

Jan and Josef continued to stay at the Ellison family home whenever they were on leave and kept in regular contact even when they went away for specialist training to Scotland and parachute training in Manchester. Lorna said that whenever the men slept in the family blue room they always made a point of sleeping with revolvers under their pillow. "In some books it talks about the men having their guns in a wicker basket", said Lorna, "but I distinctly remember taking them a cup of tea one morning to wake them up. I saw the guns under their pillows. When I asked about them Jan said there were a lot of Fifth Columnists about and they couldn't take any chances." (Fifth Columnists were German spies in Britain.)

Lorna was also at pains to tell me how in many books it talks about Josef's quick temper but that she never ever saw him lose his temper, not even once. If he knocked a drink over he would have been more inclined to laugh about it and then apologise.

Once the men were moved from Cholmondeley Castle and were stationed at Moreton Paddox near Leamington Spa, they continued to stay in touch by sending cards and, in the case of Josef, sometimes cheeky notes. Many of the people in Whitchurch had befriended members of the Czechoslovak Brigade and on one occasion they organised a coach trip to visit the men in their new barracks. The two Ellison girls, Edna and Lorna went on this trip, together with their mother Jessie, to visit Jan and Josef. Lorna remembers it was a day after Coventry had been heavily bombed by the Luftwaffe. Jan and Josef organised a taxi and all five of them went on a trip to see the damage that German bombs had caused.

After Moreton Paddox, Jan had injured his ankle on manoeuvres and he came to stay on his own, to rest up. Shortly after, Jan got a telegram telling him he had to report to a secret place. (Almost certainly, this was after Karel Svoboda, who was supposed to accompany Josef Gabcik in Operation Anthropoid, injured himself taking part in a training parachute jump in early October 1941. Jan Kubis was drafted in to replace him, on the fateful mission.)

Lorna said that it was all very tearful. The whole family were upset and so was Jan, who tried to reassure the Ellisons by saying "Try not to worry, we'll be okay". He also reminded the family of the promise that Jan and Josef had made, which was once the war was over, Jan and Josef would take all the Ellison family to Prague to show them just how beautiful it was. That was the last the Ellison family ever saw, or had contact with, Jan Kubis and Josef Gabcik.

At no time had the two soldiers ever spoken of any secret mission to the Ellison family. They were all aware that the men were being specially trained but all the soldiers ever said was that they were soon to be parachuted back to Czechoslovakia and that their job was going to be to "help the underground Resistance to fight the Germans."

Sometime prior to this, Jan Kubis had presented Lorna's elder sister Edna with a beautiful ring. Lorna remembers that it had diamonds in it. Edna was absolutely delighted to receive such a gift. It looked like an engagement ring but Jan said it was a 'Remembrance Ring', to remember him by.

When the soldiers left the Ellison family home, they were obviously planning to return. They had left a number of uniforms and other personal items in the wardrobe in the "blue room". At the end of the War, the Ellison family received a telegram stating that soldiers would be calling for the items, which is exactly what happened. Armed soldiers arrived at the house and took away all the belongings of the 2 brave soldiers and the family were only left with memories.

The family always promised themselves that one day they would fulfill Jan and Josef's wishes for them all to visit Prague. Unfortunately it never happened. Happily in 2006, with the help of a British newspaper *"The Mail on Sunday"*, I was able to take Lorna to Prague to visit the places connected to Operation Anthropoid. (See Lorna's story part 2)

Reich Protector

Heydrich breezed into Prague on 27th September 1941 and so began an unprecedented reign of intimidation and terror against the Czechs. It was masterminded by Heydrich with the utmost skill and attention to the smallest detail.

Heydrich, the expert organiser, rolled into town, determined to smash any resistance or protest to German rule, which had clearly started to grow under the 63 year old von Neurath. Heydrich was determined to show the Czechs who who their master was and that only German interests counted. He was fully intent on incorporating the country into the Reich. He was willing to use his "carrot and stick" method, or indeed, any method that brought about results, even if it included cruelty, terror, fear, torture and murder.

Upon his arrival in Prague, even before he was officially installed as leader, Heydrich announced by radio bulletins and blood-red posters that martial law was to be set up. On the very first day of Heydrich's leadership, the Czech Prime Minister Alois Elias was arrested on the basis that there was evidence to prove that Elias had been in regular radio contact with London. Heydrich wasted no time and within a few days Elias was tried and sentenced to death.

The official inauguration ceremony of Heydrich took place on September 28th 1941, starting at 11am, in the grounds of Prague's historic Hradcany castle, under the now-flying flag of the SS. The ceremony showed that Prague was now an SS State. It was obvious to anyone that Heydrich, if necessary, intended to rule the Protectorate with an iron fist.

Heydrich takes office at Hradcany Castle

He immediately instigated the combing of the Czech lands for Jews to send to concentration camps and ordered the closing of all Synagogues. He set up a holding and transportation camp at Terezin just north of Prague. This would soon become a fully fledged concentration camp.

As von Neurath had left his post on the pretext of illness, Heydrich was never officially the Reich Protector. His title would be *Acting* Reich Protector of Bohemia and Moravia but he was not going to let a trivial matter like that stand in his way. To all intents and purposes he was the Reich Protector and woe betide anyone or anything that stood in his way. He was Adolf Hitler's personal representative in the Protectorate and to him that was all that mattered.

Heydrich enters the Castle

Shortly after taking office, Heydrich made a speech in which he outlined his intentions. He said that *".... all Czechs must know that they belong to the Reich"* and that they *".... owe their allegiance to the Reich"*. He went on to say *"I need peace in this region, so that every Czech worker can work to his maximum for the German war effort"*. He is later quoted from the same speech as saying that there was a second task that must remain secret for now, which he would fulfill. *"Those who are racially inferior will be got rid of and there is plenty of room for them in the East."*

Heydrich outlines his plans

Heydrich's deputy in Prague was a ruthless former book-keeper from the Sudetenland, SS Gruppenfuhrer Karl Hermann Frank. Frank, who was already in Prague as the Reich Protector's State Secretary, actually harboured hopes of taking over from von Neurath but he soon dropped any resentment he may have felt over Heydrich's appointment and became a more-than willing accomplice in the terror campaign.

Master and his Deputy Karl Hermann Frank

Heydrich's methods soon started to produce results. He slammed down hard on the black- market dealers. Many were executed and their goods distributed to the factory workers. It was the same scenario with farmers who had previously been presenting falsified quota figures.

Heydrich, being a brilliant and cunning manipulator, *with a mind and mentality of a modern computer,* also looked at the situation in the factories. After somewhat insincere discussions with union leaders, he ordered the setting up of factory canteens, increased wages, rations, pensions and social security. He even had thousands of pairs of free shoes distributed to the workers. The measures were well received and production increased dramatically in the armaments factories. The added measure of bumper crops from the farms was also a bonus. This was a disastrous situation for the Allies and especially for Benes and his Government-in-Exile.

The Benes Government in London was being humiliated and losing a lot of credibility. Through radio broadcasts, the exiled Czechs urged the Resistance movement to act against the German occupiers but this was largely falling on deaf ears. There was no doubt now that the workforce had been tamed by Heydrich using his "carrot" strategy. His SS and Gestapo had great success in smashing the resistance reaping huge results for Heydrich's "stick" method. Clearly, a peace of sorts had taken over Bohemia and Moravia since Heydrich's arrival. This situation could not be allowed to continue, and something had to be done.

Though the Czech Resistance had been largely quelled by Heydrich's Gestapo, a secret radio message that was sent from Prague on 3rd February 1942 dramatically sums up the feeling of the Czech population inside the Protectorate. The radio message claimed that "...*apart from paid servants of the Germans, every single Czech feels the most violent hate of everything that is German. We restrict ourselves to clenched teeth and fists, and wait for the moment when the whole thing will crack. Then it will be terrible. At the first sign that the end is approaching, the whole nation will hurl itself into a general movement.*"

Anthropoid

Due to the high cost of Operation Anthropoid, accepting responsibility for it has always been a contentious issue. President Benes always denied knowing anything about it until it was too late. However, most researchers today feel that in making this claim Benes was possibly playing the game of politics. Certainly, I have seen a Top Secret Special Operations Executive memo which is available in the UK National Archives ref; HS4/39 323709 and in it it states that *"... to begin with President Benes was somewhat apprehensive of the possible repercussions in the Protectorate, but that on second thoughts he has decided that it will stimulate the will to resist at home and gain the Czechs much credit abroad, and was well worth it."* This was written on 30/5/1942 by a top British Military Intelligence officer

The situation in the Czech lands was becoming disastrous for the Benes Government. It was also disastrous for the Allies in most of the European theatre of war. So much so, that Winston Churchill had earlier set up a sabotage organisation in Britain called the Special Operations Executive or S.O.E. for short. This special unit was designed to use any means possible to weaken the German war effort. At the time resistance to German rule was down to a trickle, with factory machines humming and record production levels being posted. The underground movement's best people were being rounded up, imprisoned or executed and clandestine radio transmitters were being shut down. A small number of parachutists were dropped into the Protectorate, but they were being quickly rounded-up as the population were so in fear of the Gestapo, that any active help was reduced to a minimum. Britain and Russia were relegating the Benes Government to a very minor position and this Government in Exile realised that a spark was going to be needed to activate the mass of the Czech population.

Some years after the war, the head of the Czech military intelligence team based partly in Porchester Gate, on Bayswater Road, London, Colonel Frantisek Moravec wrote his memoirs and it contained some dramatic facts. He wrote that in discussions with President Benes he had pointed out that Anthropoid would cost lives. He went on to write, that for the good of the country, Benes ordered Moravec to proceed with the attack on Heydrich. Moravec also wrote that the day before Gabcik and Kubis were flown out, they had had an audience with President Benes where Benes stressed the historical importance of the mission to the two soldiers and became quite emotional. Moravec wrote that when the meeting was over Benes had tears in his eyes. Benes's private secretary, Dr Eduard Taborsky, wrote in his diary that the evening before Gabcik and Kubis were flown out, two young men had visited Benes for a private audience. At the time Taborsky didn't know who they were but he believed later it was Jan and Josef. (I have also seen a special invitation card from Benes and his wife, for Josef Gabcik to have tea with them. Why was Josef invited and did he keep the appointment? If so, what was discussed? Perhaps we'll never know.)

It must have been a massive weight of guilt to Benes and in no way is this book a criticism of him. It is often disputed who ordered Anthropoid to be carried out and the overwhelming likelihood is that it was President Benes, with the details being then carried through by Moravec's team, who, later in life, said in a lecture in America that he was proud to have been involved. Anyway, the main point was that Anthropoid was ordered, and preparations were begun.

The vague description of the orders of Operation Anthropoid were that. *"... at the right time, and in the right place, and under ideal conditions, perform sabotage or terrorist activity, important enough that it will be well-known even outside of Czechoslovakia."* Orders deliberately vague, it has been argued, so as to provide a smokescreen of responsibility. It now certain that, with more recent evidence, the actual order was given to "get Heydrich."

Anthropoid was originally intended to leave Britain as early as October 1941. This date proved prematurely optimistic. Dates were limited for a parachute drop into the Czech lands, due to small windows of opportunity brought about by night conditions which were necessary for the long flight. These were limited to only a couple of days, either side of a full moon.

Initially, the two men chosen for the mission were Josef Gabcik and Karel Svoboda. They had been sent for rigorous specialist training but when Svoboda injured himself during a practice parachute jump, it was decided that a replacement was needed. On the urging of Gabcik, the man chosen was his best friend, Jan Kubis. This delayed the proposed date, due to Kubis having to undergo the specialist training and also because false documentation would be needed to be produced for him. Added to this was also the failure of other parachute drops such as Operation Percentage, which had tried and failed to help reconnect the radio link between London and the Czech underground.

Gabcik and Kubis used this delay to hone their training which included shooting, bomb throwing and also attacking a moving car, an old Austin, which they did under the watchful eyes of Peter Wilkinson and Alfgar Hesketh-Pritchard at Aston House, near Stevenage, Hertfordshire.

Training complete and after a couple of false starts, (it would appear that the flight was cancelled on two nights previously, the nights of 25/26 and also 26/27 December due to adverse weather forecasts) both men were flown out of Tangmere airfield on Britain's south coast, on the night of December 28th 1941. The Air Transport Operation Report of the flight gives the official log as:

Arrival at Tangmere Cottage	1515 hrs
Arrival at Tangmere Aerodrome	2140 hrs
Take Off	2202 hrs
Dropping	0230 hrs
Aircraft landing back	0811 hrs

Josef Gabcik   *Jan Kubis*

Both Warrant Officers and both decorated soldiers, best friends Josef Gabcik and Jan Kubis were on their way back home to take the fight on behalf of Czechoslovakia to the German occupiers. Both men were given cover names to use, Gabcik as Zdenek Vyskocil, and Kubis as Otto Strnad. At the time both men were a rank in the Czechoslovak army which was called "Rotmistr", a rank in a category of sergeants, not quite officers but above the rank of a sergeant.

Other parachutists went with them that same night, when the four-engine Halifax aeroplane, captained by Ronald Hockey, took off. The parachute groups Silver A and Silver B, who were to perform other missions, were to be dropped on the same night. Many of the parachute groups were given names connected to elements such as Silver, Zinc, Steel, and Tin. Anthropoid means *"like a man"* and this is even more evidence, if it was needed, to show that it was planned to deal with a man. In another National Archive document (HS4/39 323709) a report labelled Most Secret and signed by Captain Hesketh Pritchard on 22nd January 1942, states that the men were dropped with enough equipment to carry out their assignment, equipment that would enable the men to attack Heydrich by a number of alternative means. These included getting in to his castle, getting in to his office, bombing either his car or train, mining a road he was thought to be about to travel on or shooting him at some ceremony. The report goes on to say that *'the men intend to carry out the operation whether or not there is any opportunity of subsequent escape.'*

Due to heavy snow on the ground that night, the navigator had great difficulty identifying the intended drop zone. This should have been near to Borek Aerodrome in Plzen. Gabcik and Kubis were dropped from 900 foot at 2.24am, nearly 70 miles from their intended landing zone. Josef Gabcik reportedly said, as he was about to jump, *"Remember, you will be hearing from us"*.

The men landed very near to a small village called Nehvizdy, which is about 20 miles east of Prague. The landing was bad, and Josef badly sprained his ankle in the snow. He also dislocated the big toe on his left foot. It's known that the Germans were aware that parachutists had dropped in the area that very night and they tried to find them. They even sent bulletins to local police stations to be on the lookout for parachutists.

Gabcik and Kubis tried to bury their parachutes in the snow as best they could. After hiding their equipment in a nearby shed belonging to a local man, Antonin Sedlacek, they hid out in a nearby cave.

That very night they were discovered by two separate local men, who fortunately were sympathetic to the Resistance movement. This was a huge stroke of luck for the two parachutists, as any kind of active help was difficult to find in the fear-filled Protectorate. Luck was on the side of Gabcik and Kubis on that cold, December dawn.

The locals did what they could to help the paratroopers. Food, supplies and information were brought to Jan and Josef by the fearful local people as they hid in a nearby quarry. Many of the people, who helped the parachutists at this early stage, were soon to pay with their lives and the lives of their entire families.

Eventually, the two men were put in contact with the Resistance organisation, JINDRA. After reassuring the JINDRA members that they were not Agent Provocateurs, Jan and Josef were taken under their wing and made their way to Prague, where amongst other things Josef could receive medical help for his injured foot. At some stage they also visited Plzen, which was near to their intended drop zone. At first the JINDRA organisation was wary of these two strangers. In one of my favourite books on Anthropoid, "Target Heydrich" by the late Miroslav Ivanov, JINDRA leader Ladislav Vanek said he questioned Jan Kubis by asking what was extraordinary at a train station in Moravia called Vlastivav, which was near Jan's home. Straight away Jan said *"Why, the flower display of course"*, and as Vlastivav railway station was said to have a magnificent display of roses, this helped convince JINDRA that the men were who they said they were.

Within the JINDRA organisation, Gabcik and Kubis soon found themselves under the care of a schoolteacher called Jan Zelenka who worked within JINDRA under the cover name Hajsky. He found them various "safe houses". These were just small flats or apartments, where the men could stay for a few nights, living with trusted families, before being moved on to a different safe house. This was decided to be the safest way of not compromising both the parachutists and the people hiding them. Eventually, through this "safe house" system, Jan and Josef found themselves living with a brave family called the Moravecs (no relation to the Czech military intelligence leader Colonel Moravec), in their small apartment in Biskupova Street in the Zizkov district of Prague. This was exactly the same street on which Jan Zelenka lived.

Planning

Gabcik and Kubis spent several months monitoring Heydrich's movements. They were trying to plot some kind of pattern to his timetable in order to work out a possible plan of attack. In an S.O.E. Most Secret document filed in the UK National Archives, relating to Operation Anthropoid 30/5/42 (Ref HS4/39 323709) entitled 'Detailed Report' the men had been advised to get jobs as road sweepers so that on the day chosen for the attack they could start sweeping the area using their dustman's barrow to conceal their arms and explosives. However, there is no evidence to say that the men ever got such a job. Whenever they were asked what they were doing in Prague, the men liked to answer *"We are counting the ducks on the Vltava River"*. Jan Kubis's family told me that Jan met up with his father and brother, in a wood near to his home in Moravia, on a couple of occasions around this time. He didn't tell them what he was planning but he did say he was going to do something which they would hear about later. They also said that Jan's brother Jaroslav was in regular contact with Jan and even visited him in Prague.

Through Jan Zelenka, the men were able to be in regular contact with a couple of people who worked in close proximity to Heydrich. One was a man called Josef Novotny, whose job was to fix all the clocks at Hradcany Castle where Heydrich had his office and another was an odd-job maintenance man named Frantisek Safarik. Their task was to observe anything and everything they could which they could pass on as useful information. To help in the transfer of information the JINDRA organisation even installed two young ladies with the surnames Kovarnikova and Malinova, in to a nearby house in Letenska Street. This house was almost directly underneath the castle walls and messages could be passed to the girls through a window.

Gabcik and Kubis also spent many hours watching the villa that the Heydrich family had taken over at a place called Panenske Brezany. The villa was a few miles north of Prague and it is written by survivors of the time, that Josef and Jan spent many hours lying in nearby ditches watching their prey. It is also said that they returned to their "safe houses" covered in mud. Originally, one of the plans of attack being put together was to attack Heydrich as his car set off from his home, using a steel cable or rope stretched across the road to stop the car. They even went as far as getting the cable from a Resistance man who had stolen it from his work place. This plan was eventually discarded though, as it was generally open countryside near the villa, with little chance of escape and to where German soldiers could quickly reach and rescue Heydrich. Not that escape was the top priority for Gabcik and Kubis, as another of their plans discussed was to strap explosives to their bodies and throw themselves on to his car.

Eventually all this monitoring and plotting paid dividends. Most days, Heydrich was chauffeur-driven from his villa to his office at the castle, a drive that was approximately twelve miles long. Part of this journey involved negotiating a very severe hairpin bend between Kirchmeyer Street and Holesovice, not far from the Kobylisy execution grounds. Cars would have to really slow down to take this sharp bend and the men decided that this would give them the opportunity they were looking for. It was also near to a tram stop, which meant that the men could wait around without looking too suspicious.

They returned to their various safe houses where they started to plan the finer details of the operation. Whilst at the Moravec family house they were joined by another "guest" of the family. He was a parachutist who had been dropped the same December night as part of a different mission, code-named Silver A. His name was Josef Valcik and

Josef Valcik

he'd been forced to go on-the-run when the Gestapo discovered him working as a waiter in a hotel called Hotel Veselka in Pardubice. Josef and Jan realised they could use Valcik's help and so he was recruited into the plan.

While they were planning the attack, the parachutists were greatly helped by the JINDRA organisation. It organised people to supply them with snippets of information and also organised the provision of safe havens for the parachutists. Brave families included the Moravecs, the Novaks, the Svatos, the Fafeks, the Khodls and the Ogouns, plus other families and people who will forever remain nameless. The vast majority of these families paid with their lives for the help and assistance they gave.

The plan was eventually formulated. Valcik would be the look-out. When the car was approaching he would signal, using a small mirror to catch the sun, to Gabcik who would be waiting on the sharp bend with a gun.

Normally, where Heydrich went, so too did his SS security guards. A code to confirm the presence of security guards was hatched. It was simple - "hat on" if there were bodyguards with Heydrich, and "hat off" if it was just him and his chauffeur. With a love for speed, Heydrich would often get his chauffeur to overtake the slow-moving troop carriers and so it was important to know if this could make him more vulnerable. There were later reports that a car carrying Resistance workers was to drive past the men waiting on the bend, with people in the car either wearing or not wearing hats as the signal, but I have yet to see sufficient evidence to convince me of this.

All was now ready. Preparations were complete. Once the signal came from Valcik's mirror, announcing the arrival of Heydrich's car, Gabcik would reveal a Sten machine gun, step forward and shoot the Acting Reich Protector. Jan Kubis would be placed just a little further on, hoping to snatch Heydrich's briefcase but also armed with a couple of primed grenade-type bombs in case they were needed, bombs that were primed to explode on impact regardless of how they landed. The theory was perfect. Now it had to be implemented.

The night before the attack

Assassination

Wednesday 27th May 1942 was a beautiful sunny day in Prague, 7 months to the day since Heydrich arrived. The weather signalled that summer was truly here and, who knows, maybe the start of good things for the city.

Josef Gabcik and Jan Kubis were up and out early. They had work to do today. The previous night had been spent sleeping at the Ogoun's safe-house, in Vaclavkova Street in Dejvice, on the outskirts of Prague. As they left the house that morning, Josef had said to Josef Ogoun *"Don't worry if we are not back as usual"*. The men carried briefcases, with Josef also carrying a beige raincoat. It looked to all the world as if they were just two people going to work. Of course they were going to work…but it was work with a difference.

They collected their bicycles, which they had stored in a nearby garage and rode off with their briefcases strapped to the handlebars. Eventually they reached the sharp hairpin bend in the Liben district, just to the north of the city. There they dismounted and propped the bikes up against some nearby lamp-posts. They would be needed soon enough.

Here, as arranged, Josef and Jan met up with other men. One was Josef Valcik, with his signalling mirror; the other was parachutist Adolf Opalka. He had been dropped as part of the OUT DISTANCE group, whose job was to try to restore communications between London and the underground network. After a short "conflab", each man went to his designated starting position.

Adolf Opalka

Valcik went to the approach road. It has never been confirmed but I believe the approach road, Kirchmeyer Street, had other lookout men posted to let Valcik know to give the signal. My theory comes from knowing the terrain from visits and studying maps of the time. I don't believe Valcik would have had much time to signal to the corner, from where he was placed, by the time the car came into his view. Certainly, there is some evidence to suggest that other Resistance people were mobilised that day to go to various points in the vicinity of the attack scene. Their job may have been to use delaying tactics by asking the police questions and divert them from their security tasks.

Opalka went to his start position across the road. Again, it's never been officially confirmed but I believe Opalka's specific job was to cross the road at the right time in order to make Heydrich's car slow down even more than it had to. Opalka was the highest-ranking of the parachutist, and so, to a certain extent, could have had some authority at the scene. Josef Gabcik took up his position on the pavement, right in the middle of the curve and just out of sight of any approaching car. Josef held on tight to his briefcase. A quick glance inside would have revealed the case to be full of grass cuttings. At the time, people were allowed to breed rabbits for food and so they were permitted to collect grass from parklands to feed them with. A policeman or passing security officer might accept that Josef's case was being used for this purpose. A closer look, however, would reveal that underneath the grass was a Sten machine gun, modified with the shoulder support cut off and the rest of the gun broken down in to three separate parts. Josef had rigorously practised assembling and reassembling this machine gun. He was so adept at this, he could do it with his eyes closed. He would be doing it again very soon, before Heydrich's car approached.

Jan Kubis was placed a bit further round the corner than Josef, waiting to pounce on Heydrich's document folder. He was also there as a back-up and/or to deal with any bodyguards. He had his hand-held bombs ready in his briefcase.

They had gone over the plan so many times; they had worked it out to the second. No one was in any doubt as to their role in the mission. All they needed to do now was to wait. Not too long now. It was 9 o'clock and 9.30am would soon be here, the time that Heydrich's car usually approached the bend..

Meanwhile, at Heydrich's villa in Panenske Brezany, the chauffeur Johannes Klein had arrived promptly. He dare not be late, today of all days, as Heydrich may be flying out for a meeting with the Fuhrer in Berlin. The Acting Reich Protector had achieved great results in Bohemia and Moravia and it may be time for a change, France perhaps? Maybe the Fuhrer would confirm this today? At last, his grizzly and brutal talents could be properly recognised.

"I'm flying to Berlin" he may have told his family, as they strolled through the grounds of the villa. He played with his three children for a short while and spoke to his wife Lina who was heavily pregnant with their fourth child. Heydrich liked to visit the Nazi brothels and had even set up his own brothel in Berlin called Salon Kitty. This was done with the intention of recording pillow talk from its many high-ranking guests. He had secret microphones put in the rooms and recording equipment in the basement. It is said that whenever he made a visit the microphones were switched off! However, his wife had done him and the party mantra proud by producing children, and this is what could have been going through his mind that morning.

Heydrich almost had a reluctance to leave home that morning. Helena Vovsova, the gardener at the Heydrich's villa, told me that on the morning in question she saw him lift his daughter up in his arms, which was very unusual. Did he have some kind of premonition of the fate awaiting him? The chauffeur standing alongside the gleaming Mercedes kept looking at his watch.

Eventually, nearly an hour later than normal, Heydrich gathered up his official papers and climbed into the front passenger seat. As the chauffeur closed the door, Heydrich placed his overcoat on the rear seat but he clung on to his briefcase. That would stay on his knee for the duration of the journey. "At last" thought the chauffeur Klein, as the dark green, open-topped Mercedes 320, pulled away, around the side of the house, and up the drive.

Today as Heydrich was running unusually late, he urged the chauffeur to speed up, even though it meant leaving the guards lagging behind. He felt safe in Prague. None of the Czechs would be brave enough to attack him and, besides, he'd increased their wages and living conditions, so why would he fear them? Klein heard the urgency in Heydrich's order and he must have thought how pleased he had been, that the recent proposal from the Fuhrer to have heavy armour plating installed on the car and inside the seats had been ignored. That would have slowed them down considerably. Now he could step on the gas of the open topped Mercedes. Pedestrians and bicycles would soon get out of the way once they saw Heydrich's pennant on the wing of the car.

At the sharp corner, the parachutists waited. Heydrich was normally due by 9.30am, but at 10 o'clock the men were still waiting. A quick meeting ended with Josef urging the others to be patient. Was it a trap? Was Heydrich not coming? Would they be noticed as loitering? All sorts of things must have been racing through the minds of the waiting soldiers. At ten past ten there was no Heydrich. Ten fifteen, no Heydrich. Ten twenty, no Heydrich. The tension must have been unbearable.

Suddenly, at ten thirty, *the mirror caught the sun*. Heydrich's car was approaching. It is also possible that Valcik, as well as using the hand-held mirror to signal the approach, also blew a loud whistle. That is what some passers-by reported. This was also the signal, I believe, for Josef Gabcik to move a bit further around the corner, to take up his position so he wouldn't be sighted until the Mercedes slowed down. Importantly, but not make-or-break for the operation, the car was approaching and there was a "no hat" signal, meaning no security guards were in attendance.

All the training, all the hiding and the planning came down to this moment. This is it!

As the car slowed to take the sharp curve, I believe Opalka crossed the road, a crossing timed to make the Mercedes slow down even more than it had to. This is not normally mentioned in most accounts of the attack but Opalka was there at the scene and he would have had a part to play.

The car slowed to around 15mph. As it came around the corner, Josef Gabcik threw down the long beige raincoat he'd borrowed for the very purpose and revealed his modified, and now assembled, Sten machine gun. On sight of the car, he stepped off the kerb, aimed the gun, absolutely could not miss, pulled the trigger..........and nothing happened.

Unbelievably, the gun had jammed.

Chaos

Josef was frantic. It had all depended on that split second, and now a technical malfunction. After meticulous planning and utmost bravery who would have thought this could happen? Split seconds must have seemed like hours. Could a fault with the gun have caused it to jam? After all, the Sten gun was notoriously unreliable, cheap and mass-produced? Yes, it's possible, even probable to some.

Theories abound as to why the gun didn't function, including Josef deliberately not shooting as he saw the number 3 tram approaching and he would have realised that innocent people could be injured. Another theory centred around Josef dating a religious-minded woman who he knew wouldn't be happy with him shooting someone! Personally, I discount these theories as not being creditable. Could Josef have assembled the Sten gun wrongly, or even left a safety catch on? Highly unlikely. Even under the extreme pressure of action, this is what Josef had trained for. He could do it blindfolded. It was Josef who broke it down into three parts in his briefcase and then covered it with grass cuttings. The grass cuttings?

Wet grass cuttings and mechanisms surely don't make a good match. It is possible that this is the most likely explanation. In his efforts to conceal the gun from suspicious eyes, I suspect the most likely cause of the gun jamming at the crucial time is that a few blades of grass got mixed up in the firing mechanism. Surely Operation Anthropoid, planned for nearly a year, could not fail because of a few grass cuttings?

As Josef pulled on the gun with manic urgency and with panic sweat covering his face, the chauffeur made a fatal mistake. Instead of doing what trained bodyguards are supposed to do in a situation like this, trying to speed away, Klein hit the brakes. They'd seen Josef and, more importantly, they'd seen the gun aimed straight at them. They couldn't miss it from only a few feet away. Klein later said it was Heydrich who shouted to him to stop. As the car slowed, Heydrich who was sat nearest the kerb jumped up from his seat and grabbed his pistol. What he didn't know, couldn't know, and probably didn't see in the excitement, was a second man, waiting just a bit further on.

In an instant, Jan Kubis, almost staring in disbelief at the scene, snapped in to action. He grabbed a grenade from his briefcase and tossed it underarm, as he'd been trained to do at Aston House, at the car. The grenade, modified to explode on impact, missed the inside of the car. Instead, it caught the bottom of the back half of the bodywork.

Boom! It exploded, and now the whole area was in total chaos. The number 3 tram stopping nearby caught some of the blast, causing many of its windows to smash and some passengers to get injured. Jan himself was injured too. Some of the shrapnel embedded itself in his face and chest. The explosion caused damage to the rear of the car, as the Mercedes lurched to an ugly stop. It's reported that the two grey leather SS overcoats that had been placed on the back seat of the car, ended up on the tram lines overhead.

The scene of Operation Anthropoid

The damaged car

The damage to the car was mostly all on one side

Heydrich jumped from the car. Bystanders say he fired his pistol at Kubis, but Klein said he'd forgotten to load his gun, so this couldn't be. Those few seconds were utter chaos. Suddenly, Heydrich slumped, clutching his back. A piece of shrapnel from the blast had pierced the rear of Heydrich's seat, (the same seat that had not had the armour plating added as the Fuhrer's office had advised) and had actually punctured Heydrich's lower back. In the chaos of the moment, Jan Kubis, his face now covered with blood from his wounds, threw his briefcase over some nearby railings. He managed to reach his bicycle, which he'd left nearby and pedalled furiously away from the scene, firing his own pistol in the air to help make good his escape. He made his way to the Novak safe house in the Liben district.

Josef Gabcik meanwhile, threw down his now useless machine gun and ran off, back up Kirchmeyer Street, in the direction from which the Mercedes had come. Klein rushed to help his injured boss. Through gritted teeth, Heydrich pointed to the fleeing Gabcik and said *"Get that bastard"*.

Klein chased Josef down a couple of streets, streets that are now named in honour of the parachutists: Gabcikova, Kubisova, and Valcikova.

It is actually said that a wild west style chase ensued with Gabcik and Klein exchanging shots. However, Klein later told the Gestapo investigation that he had inadvertently pressed the gun's magazine release catch, so he couldn't shoot. Josef, in his haste, spotted a butcher's shop, Brauners. He raced inside, hoping to escape through a back door. Unfortunately for him, there was no back door. Even worse, Brauner the butcher was a Nazi sympathiser and he ran out and spotted Klein approaching out of breath. *"He's in there,"* shouted Brauner, and pointed to the door.

The butcher's shop which Josef Gabcik ran into

At virtually the same time, Josef realising his mistake, burst out of the door and nearly collided with the chauffeur, who was now crouching behind a nearby post. Josef managed to shoot the chauffeur in the leg and ran off. A witness said his escape saw him running frantically, with his tie flying in the wind and then saw him jump over some small railings, through a garden, and away into the city, where he eventually ended up at the Fafek family safe house, in the Vinohrady district of Prague.

Back at the scene of the explosion, a crowd had gathered to watch the injured Heydrich. A blonde female passer-by called Marie Navarova managed to flag down a passing Tatra van that was doing its rounds delivering floor polish. Heydrich was placed in the van, first in the front, and then face down in the back, atop boxes of floor wax and polish, and taken to the nearby Bulovka Hospital, by the reluctant driver, a man by the name of Frantisek Sitta. (Later reports have Marie Navarova in the pay of the Gestapo. A Czech magazine article claimed she was sent to prison after the war for being an informant.)

Meanwhile, back at the villa at Panenske Brezany, word soon came about the attack. The gardener Helena Vovsova told me that there was a big rush of soldiers, running about and shouting. Helena also saw Lina Heydrich staring out of the window crying. She saw the German man who looked after the horses on the estate and asked "What's going on?". He replied, "There was an assassination attempt on the Chief". She asked "Is he dead?" and the reply came "Not yet".

Helena and the staff were terrified that day, as they all wondered what would become of them if they were under suspicion of having helped.

Bulovka

Heydrich was stripped to the waist by the time the duty-Doctor arrived. He was obviously in great pain, yet he allowed the doctor to prod and push the wound with his swabs. The doctor tried to clean it and examine it as best as he could but an X-ray was required. Heydrich walked to the machine, grimacing but upright. The hospital receptionist on duty that day also testified that Heydrich walked in to the hospital. He said that he was very pale when he slowly entered the hospital.

The X-ray revealed the extent of the damage, mostly to the left of Heydrich's spine. A piece of shrapnel, according to the first Gestapo report, had "smashed a rib, punctured the stomach, and lodged itself in the spleen". The thoracic cage was blown open and, most worryingly, other foreign debris, most notably parts of the car seat had penetrated into the wound. There was a serious risk of septicaemia. (Initial reports in England led the Allied authorities to believe Heydrich had also suffered bullet wounds to his neck and back. There was even a suspicion that the bullets were of a similar calibre used by the Gestapo. Had they shot him? However, these reports have now been disregarded. On 11th February 1943 a report came in from the S.O.E. office in Stockholm to say that the Sten gun had jammed after a few shots. This is all in the UK National Archives file on Anthropoid)

A German doctor, Professor Walter Dick, had meanwhile been called to the hospital. He spoke to Heydrich and explained that an operation was immediately necessary to remove the splinters before they got the chance to fester. Heydrich at first refused, insisting that German surgeons were brought in. The German Professor Hollbaum was called from another suburb of Prague and so he helped perform the operation almost as soon as he arrived.

SS storm troopers arrived at the hospital as soon as the alert was sounded. After the operation, Heydrich was taken to a room on the second floor, a room that had been Professor Dick's office and the SS turned the whole wing in to a fortress. Czech patients in the vicinity were removed, windows were whitewashed, sentries were placed and even a machine-gun nest was set up on the roof. From now on, no Czechs were allowed near to Heydrich. Gestapo officials came and went, as did Heydrich's deputy Karl Frank. Himmler who visited twice, had his own top surgeons brought in from Berlin.

On hearing the news of the attack on Heydrich, Hitler flew in to an absolute rage. He ordered savage reprisals against the Czech population. Karl Frank declared a state of emergency. The whole area of the attack was sealed off and searched for clues. A curfew was announced on the whole of Prague and any places of entertainment were closed. It's said that the very first night, the German security forces searched over 36,000 homes but found no sign of the attackers. The Germans were raging. One man who lived through those days as a ten year old boy was Josef Pley. He told me that it was a most awful time. Even as children they were too scared to even go out to play. He said in those first few days you could get shot, just for looking wrongly at a German soldier. Another man who lived in the Pankrac district of Prague in 1942 was Karl Tosner. He remembered that at the beginning of the occupation things were relatively calm but that it all changed after Anthropoid. Everyone became terrified and whole families could disappear just for someone saying the wrong thing. People became wary of even their next door neighbour.

Meanwhile, as Heydrich lay in hospital, the attackers were certain that their attempt on the life of the Acting Reich Protector had failed.

Jan Kubis had fled the scene on his borrowed bicycle. He'd managed to make it to the Novak's safe house in the Liben district of Prague but, due to his facial injuries, he'd left the bike outside the nearby Bata shoe shop, all covered in blood. Mrs Novak sent her young daughter Jindriska to recover the bike but she was spotted. This action eventually cost the whole Novak family their lives. Josef Gabcik meanwhile, had made it safely to the Fafek's house.

The searches continued for a number of nights but still they proved fruitless. The men did what they could to alter their appearances. They dyed their hair, and grew moustaches. Execution followed execution, arrest followed arrest and threat followed threat. Big red posters were put up listing the people arrested and declaring the state of emergency. Still there was no sign of the perpetrators. Hitler's patience was wearing thin.

Meanwhile, back at the hospital, Heydrich's condition, instead of improving, had actually worsened. Though the doctors said that his chances for a full recovery were excellent, it was going seriously wrong. Heydrich developed blood poisoning, with a very high temperature. Blood transfusions were administered but these didn't help. Eventually, not too long after telling his wife Lina to take the children back to the island of Fehmarn, Heydrich, in great pain and delirious, died in his hospital bed as dawn was breaking on the morning of the 4th of June 1942. He was 38 years old. The official causes of death included septicaemia and damage of the vital organs, caused by bomb fragments, shrapnel and almost incredibly, horsehair from inside the car seat. In the hospital register, only two words described the cause of death as "wound infection". (I've read in specialist books that the bomb used to kill Heydrich was a specially modified toxin-poison bomb, the first of its kind. Jan Kubis was severely injured by the same bomb but he didn't die from it. Therefore, I don't see how the logic stands up. It makes no sense. I'm sure therefore that it was a simple case of infection that couldn't be cured.)

Funeral

The city of Prague now held its breath. Heydrich, the Acting Reich Protector, the man who tamed the Czechs was dead. After the attack Prague had already almost been sealed off from the outside world. Unless there were special circumstances no traffic was allowed in or out of the city. Now, the population feared the backlash. In a pro-Nazi demonstration in Prague the day before Heydrich died, up to 60,000 terrified people showed their supposed loyalty to the German masters.

Fresh appeals for information were constantly being made. A huge reward of ten million Czech Crowns was offered for turning over the parachutists. Items recovered at the scene, such as Josef's bicycle and beige raincoat, along with two briefcases and a cap, were put on display in a shop window at 6 Wenceslas Square, the main shopping area in the centre of Prague. *"Who knows them?"* *"Who do they belong to?"* asked the Gestapo.

The searches, the round ups and the executions continued. The 9pm to 6am curfew stayed in place. Heydrich's reign ended almost the same way it began. SS Oberstgruppenfuhrer Kurt Daluege was in the city receiving medical treatment for possible syphilis. (Though when he was on trial in Prague at the end of the war, Daluege said he raced to the city as soon as he heard the news of an attack, to see if he could help) Daluege, who was one rank higher than Heydrich, after being promoted only a month earlier, was now given the job of replacing Heydrich, once again thwarting the ambitions of Karl Frank. Daluege was a man whose intelligence was frowned upon by his fellow officers; so much so, they nicknamed him the "donkey". Perhaps he wasn't first choice, as Hitler had threatened the Czechs he would send a man called SS Gruppenfuhrer Eric von dem Bach-Zelewski, a man who would not be afraid to *"wade through blood"*. Bach-Zelewski had earned a fearsome reputation for the terrible way he had dealt with Partisans in other occupied countries like Russia and Poland. Daluege, who at the time was head of the uniformed police force throughout the Third Reich, was convinced that the attack on Heydrich was the start of a large-scale Czech rebellion towards the Germans.

After an autopsy, Heydrich's body was transferred from the hospital to Hradcany Castle. This was done at midnight, in an elaborate torchlight procession staged by the SS. The next day the coffin was laid in state in the courtyard of the castle, in front of the Matthias Gate, right under the shadow of a huge Iron Cross, erected for the very purpose. Thousands upon thousands thronged through the gates to pay their respects and salute the coffin, though it's believed many did this out of fear rather than sympathy. Also, a death mask was made of Heydrich, which one onlooker described as having *"perverted beauty, like a Cardinal of the Renaissance."*

IM NAMEN DES FÜHRERS

LADET DER

REICHSFÜHRER ⚡ UND CHEF DER DEUTSCHEN POLIZEI

ZUR TRAUERFEIER AUF DER PRAGER BURG

FÜR DEN GEFALLENEN CHEF DER SICHERHEITSPOLIZEI UND DES SD
UND STELLVERTRETENDEN REICHSPROTEKTOR IN BÖHMEN UND MÄHREN

⚡-OBERGRUPPENFÜHRER UND GENERAL DER POLIZEI
REINHARDHEYDRICH

ZU SONNTAG, DEN 7. JUNI 1942, 18 UHR, EIN

Diese *Einladung gilt als Eintrittskarte*

Die Plätze im Ehrenhof der "Burg müssen spätestens 17p'r eingenommen sein. Auffahrt von der Burgrampe. Etwaige Kranzspenden sind bis spätestens 16 Uhr in der Burg abzugeben. Trauergäste, die an dem Marsch zum Bahnhof nicht teilnehmen, werden gebeten, den Burghof vorzeitig zu verlassen. Anzug für Waffen ⚡ und Gliederungen: Großer Vieraranzug, kleine Ordensschnalle, Tätze, umgeschnallt Pistole, graue Handschuhe, weiße Wäsche,

The invitation card to Heydich's Memorial Service at Hradcany Castle
(the dress code is given as "best suit, grey gloves, white shirt and small pistol around the waist")

Thousands file past the coffin

St Katherine's Church in Grossenbrode where the Heydrichs were married

The villa in Wannsee. Heydrich chaired the conference for the
"Final Solution to the Jewish problem" here

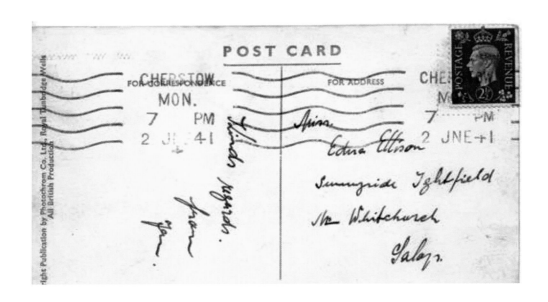

Above and below, postcards sent by Jan Kubis

Postcard sent by Josef Gabcik

Christmas card sent by Jan Kubis to the Ellison family

Did JINDRA ask Jan Kubis what was special about Vladislav train station?

I was pleased to find Heydrich's former gardner Helena Vovsova. Heydrich was driven through these gates and turned left on the fateful day of Anthropoid

The death mask made of SS Obergruppenfuhrer Reinhard Heydrich

43

The crypt of the church where seven parachutists were hidden

Once this staircase was revealed the battle for the crypt was over

The Memorial to the fallen children of Lidice.
The statue was made by Marie Uchytilova, who sadly didnt live
to see the finished product in bronze.

I studied every name on a memorial at the Kobylisy execution ground.
Nearby is a memorial plaque saying
"Stop a little while. Although our blood has been spilt in our land, we again have risen high"

The execution room at Plotzensee Prison, Berlin. Czechoslovak Resistance members were amongst the many who lost their lives here

The Memorial which includes the names of the Kubis family who lost their lives after Anthropoid

MINISTERSTVO NARODNI OBRANY.
Hlavní štáb - 2. oddělení.

Prague, August 3rd 1945.

NO:358/zvl.skup.1945

Dear Miss E l l i s o n ,

          I take the opportunity to inform you with deep regret that Lt.Jan KUBIŠ and Lt.Josef GABČÍK are reported dead.They both were killed in action in Prague on June the 18th 1942.

          They have left some of their personal things with you,and I suggest to you,knowing the transport difficulties,to send them to "Czech.Military Mission in G.B.,42,Wilton Crescent,London,S.W.1." with a note that they should be sent to G.H.Q.,2nd Dptmt in Prague for František KUBIŠ or František Gabčik respectively.In case that you prefer to send them yourself,here are the necessary addresses:Mr.František KUBIŠ,
                    Dolní Vilémovice,71,
                    pp.Lipnik u Hrotovic
                    Czechoslovakia.

and   Mr.František GABČÍK,
          Poluvsie,
             pp.Rajecké Teplice,
             Slovakia,
             Czechoslovakia.

          With many thanks I am yours sincerely

                    Col.K.P a l e č e k,
                    chief,spec.group.,
                    2nd Dptmt,G.H.Q.

To: Miss Edna E l l i s o n ,
      Sunnyside Igasfield,
      Whitchurch,
        Salop,
        England.

The official notification received by the Ellison family of the death of their "dear Czech friends"

I explained to Lorna what happened at the ventilator shaft outside the church crypt

Lorna and I looked through the personal photograph album of Jan Kubis. Lorna was delighted to see pictures of her family which Jan had called "My English Family".

The Memorial Parade at St Cyrils. Lorna and I paid our respects while Colonel Veis saluted.

I was honoured to meet the nephew of Jan Kubis, Jiri Dusik. Jiri was imprisoned after Anthropoid as a potential threat to the Nazis. He was one year old at the time!

Memorial to Josef Gabcik in Zilina. I'm pictured with Josef's relative Katarina Tomcikova

A fountain memorial to Operation Anthropoid in the shape of a parachute in Leamington Spa's Jephson Gardens, England.

Lina keeps the name Heydrich on her gravestone

The plaque on the corner of the former Gestapo headquarters in Prague, telling of the building's sinister past and urging the people to be aware!

I was delighted when Heider Heydrich (left) agreed to talk to me.

I was able to show Heider the house in Prague that the Heydrichs had lived. He'd not been for 63 years! This is us outside the gates through which his father had been driven.

I sign the visitors book in the Town Hall of Dolni Vilemovice, the home village of Jan Kubis. Colonel Frantisek Veis looks on.

The Memorial at the shooting grounds of Pardubice. The people of Lezaky were amongst those shot here.

The fencing statue presented to Reinhard Heydrich on 29th July 1936 by his SS fencing comrades.

The collectable figures of the Assassination, made by a company called King and Country

That night, after a service attended by Himmler in the courtyard and another large procession through the city, Heydrich's coffin was laid on a special train and taken to Berlin. There, the Nazis put on probably the biggest funeral in their entire history, with Hitler attending, and giving Heydrich posthumously the highest Nazi award possible, the highest decoration of the German Order, only the second person ever to receive this after Minister of Works Fridtz Todt.

Hitler salutes at the Berlin funeral

The now-widowed Lina, was not able to attend due to her being heavily pregnant but as Hitler patted the cheeks of their two young sons he said *"Heydrich, there was a man with a heart of iron"*.

Hitler greets Klaus and Heider Heydrich

The coffin was then taken on its last journey, and laid to rest in the Invaliden Military Cemetery in Berlin. It was marked by a simple white wooden cross, with elaborate plans for a future memorial but today the grave is unmarked and unidentifiable.

Now it was time for revenge.

Reprisal

Even people, who don't know about Heydrich, or his assassination, may well know the name Lidice.

One of the most sickening of a catalogue of crimes against humanity, connected to the Nazis, was the crime against Lidice.

The Nazis wanted revenge, and they wanted blood. Several captured parachutists had, under torture, mentioned addresses in Lidice and so this small village was already under suspicion. But then came perhaps, the final straw for the Gestapo concerning Lidice. One young man, anxious to let a lady be impressed that he was, falsely, a member of the Czech Resistance, wrote a letter to her in which he made very vague hints of the "fatal day", and that he was "going to disappear". The letter ended up in the wrong hands. In the white-heat confusion of those weeks, it was wrongly interpreted to be a link to the assassination. The Gestapo traced the writer of the letter, a man by the name of Vaclav Riha, and the intended recipient, Anna Maruscakova. Under interrogation, the name of Lidice, and two families living there, who both had sons serving with the RAF, were mentioned. (The Horak family and the Stribrny family) From the original evidence found at the scene of Heydrich's attack, the Gestapo already knew that Anthropoid was a British-involved operation, or as the Gestapo investigator said at the time, *"was made in England"*. In a Gestapo report dated 4 June 1942 it says that *"...other firearms found bore the marks Geco and Kyno. The guilt of England and her paid agent Benes, in the assault of Heydrich is, therefore, clearly and indisputably established"*.

The Gestapo now looked closely at this small mining village called Lidice. Unable to find any useful links in any of their other enquiries, they now believed they had found a trace to the parachutists. Previously, it had also been reported that several arrested parachutists had been given addresses in Lidice, as well as other places, as possible safe havens, and this had been carefully noted by the Gestapo. However, there is no evidence to say parachutists had actually used Lidice. It would appear that the Gestapo, with flimsy evidence, had simply wanted to use Lidice as an example to terrorise the Czech population as a whole. The order came from Hitler himself, who announced that he would be patient no more with the Czech people. He ordered the complete destruction of the village. Karl Frank said *"where Lidice stands now, I want to see corn growing within twelve months."*

On the 9th of June 1942, the Germans, led by SS Captain Max Rostock, surrounded Lidice. All 173 males over the age of 15 were rounded up and taken to a cellar belonging to a farming family called Horak. The Horak family was one of those who had a pilot son serving with the RAF.

The women and children were taken to the small schoolhouse. Every single building in Lidice was first pillaged of anything useful, and then systematically set on fire.

Early the next morning, the men were led out to an adjacent orchard on Horak's farm, in groups of ten. (It is said that there were groups of five first but this was taking too long for the Nazis and so they increased it to groups of ten) There they were lined up against a barn wall, in front of a number of propped up mattresses placed there to prevent ricochet, and shot. When one group fell, the next group were brought out, and they had to stand in a row, in front of their fellow villagers who were now dead. This continued all day, until every one of the 173 men were dead. The Mayor of Lidice was one of the last to be shot, as he had to identify his townsmen. (Another 19 Lidice men who weren't present on the tragic morning were rounded up and shot at the Prague-Kobylisy execution ground a week later, along with some female members of the Horak and Stribrny families. This group included men returning from a night-shift, one who was in hospital at the time with a broken leg and 2 boys who were discovered later to have just turned 15.)

The fallen men of Lidice

A small number of the children were considered suitable to be adopted by German families. The basic method of selection was usually by hair or eye colour. The remainder of the children and the 185 women were then sent to concentration camps. Very few of them survived the war.

The German work units now brought in to Lidice were extremely thorough. Over a period of time, they systematically levelled every single building in the village, recording some of it on movie film or having their photographs taken with the destruction in the background. The school and the church weren't spared, and neither was the graveyard. Even the small river that ran through the village was diverted from its course. Total manic revenge gone mad.

The Lidice operation was done with such thoroughness that even people who lived in the village, but weren't there on the particular day, such as a number of men who were away working, were hunted down and later shot. A couple of pregnant women from the village were taken to hospital, where they were held until they had given birth. They were then separated from their new born children and sent to concentration camps. The babies were never seen again.

Shortly afterwards, another small hamlet called Lezaky suffered a similar fate. Word had reached Gestapo headquarters that an illegal radio transmitter was operating from the nearby quarry. Because of this, Lezaky was destroyed, and the villagers were taken away to Pardubice and executed. There is evidence also, to say that other small villages such as Dolni Vilemovice where Jan Kubis came from were earmarked to suffer a similar fate, but the worldwide revulsion to these crimes perhaps made the Germans think again.

In late June 1942, the USA Secretary of the Navy Frank Knox made a speech where he said *"If future generations ask us what we were fighting for, we should tell them the story of Lidice. We will not end this war until all who are responsible, directly or indirectly, for the events of Lidice, are obliterated from the earth".*

A member of the Czech Government in London was heard to say *"A worse thing has never happened since the Dark Ages"*

Lidice before ....and after

Sanctuary

Even before Heydrich had died, the parachutists were in severe need of a proper place to hide. With the house searches continuing at an unprecedented rate, the chances of them staying undetected were slim. They were also putting at grave risk the people who were hiding them. Other parachutists, dropped for different missions, were also hiding in the city which made the problem even more acute. With access out of the city denied, the Resistance movement realised that something had to be done. A church in the city's Resslova Street provided the answer. Jan Zelenka knew about the church, and eventually he spoke with the chairman of the church council, a man by the name of Jan Sonnevend, who in turn spoke to the priest Father Vladimir Petrek. After a short meeting, the priest allowed them to hide in his church, until hopefully the heat died down. The Czechoslovak Orthodox Church, St Cyril and St

Methodius, had an underground crypt running almost its entire length. It was decided that this would be the hiding place. The parachutists were brought in at intervals, with Jan Kubis being first to arrive on the 30th May and Josef Gabcik the last on 1st June.

Altogether, seven parachutists were brought in and hidden in the underground crypt. Whilst it was far from comfortable, it was hopefully beyond the suspicions of the Gestapo. It would certainly do until a plan could be hatched to take the men out of Prague. Already, the underground movement, JINDRA, had started looking at ways of helping the men escape, ways which included smuggling them to safety in coffins. One parachutist was missing though. His name was Karel Curda, who'd been dropped as part of the OUT DISTANCE mission. After the attack on Heydrich, Curda had managed to escape from the city and was hiding in his mother's barn in southern Bohemia, in Nova Hlina near Trebon.

The underground crypt was cold. It had been used to store coffins and bones of previous church officials from years gone by. It was small, measuring about 100 feet long, by about 10 feet wide. Part of the wall was made up of honeycomb type square niches that had contained the coffins. It was hoped that it was the perfect hiding place. The priest, the Bishop, and other church officials were all in agreement for the men to use it. Some reports even say that the church officials swore on the altar to try to protect the men and not reveal their whereabouts.

Food, supplies and newspapers were brought as often as possible and the priest, Father Petrek, is said to have counselled the men who were feeling guilty about their part in the attack, or rather the high cost of it to the Czech people. Soon though, the dark, cramped and cold conditions of the crypt also began to take its toll on the men. Whilst conditions were far from ideal, the JINDRA organisation tried to get extra warm clothing for the men, supplies of which were lowered down to them by the priest using a rope, through a small trap door which provided the only real access point. A lime-filled bucket provided the only WC facility. The men had a ladder down in the crypt and this was also utilised. The only real ventilation to the crypt though, was through a small grill high up in the crypt but at street level from the outside.

News reached the men of Heydrich's death but also about the reprisals on the population. The parachutists were at a loss. Gabcik and Kubis discussed giving themselves up to the authorities in the hope that the retributions would stop. They even considered going to a park, wearing signs around their necks announcing they were the assassins before shooting themselves. Morale was low amongst the men. Some of the parachutists, including Jan Kubis, had started to feel the effects of living in this environment and illness set in. (Kubis of course, was still suffering with his shrapnel wounds received during the bomb blast of Heydrich's car and it's said that he actually went out from the church to visit a doctor during the time of hiding there.).The men found some comfort from the oppression by taking it in turns to keep guard in the upper parts of the church, high up in the choir balcony.

Whilst the Gestapo were leaving no stone unturned in the frantic search for the parachutists, the men were, hopefully, safe for the time-being.

Betrayal

The hunt was most definitely on. Prague was sealed to the outside world; house to house searches were continuing at an incredible and manic rate. There were many arrests and executions but still the Gestapo found no sign of the parachutists. Lidice happened, and still no sign of the parachutists. Hitler was livid and threatened massive reprisals against the Czech population.

Massive rewards were announced, up to ten million Czech Crowns for the right information. The Gestapo received many bits of information but much of it was false and deliberately designed to put the Gestapo off the scent.

The person put in charge of the Gestapo investigation was a man called Heinz von Panwitz. He looked at all the threats towards the population and he felt that these were actually having a negative affect on people coming forward with information. Fear was running throughout Prague and it wasn't helping the Gestapo. So, together with Karl Frank, he came up with a plan that offered amnesty and safety to anyone coming forward.

As Hitler announced plans to have thirty thousand Czechs rounded up and shot in retaliation, the amnesty was announced. Hitler reluctantly agreed to it and the Gestapo awaited the results. Unfortunately for the parachutists, and their helpers, the Gestapo didn't have to wait long.

Petschek Palace, the former HQ of Prague's Gestapo

On the 16th June, just before lunch, a man walked into the Gestapo headquarters at Petschek Palace, a building few Czechs ever entered voluntarily and said he had some information.

That man was the parachutist who had escaped the city on the first day, a friend of the other parachutists, Karel Curda.

The betrayer, Karel Curda

It transpired that a couple of days before, Curda had written an anonymous letter to the authorities naming Gabcik and Kubis as the perpetrators of the attack on Heydrich. Now, he'd caught the train and offered himself up to the authorities. (He said later that he couldn't stand to hear of all the purges and executions that were taking place. He said all this though, whilst spending the reward money!)

Curda admitted little at first. He said he recognised the briefcases that were found at the scene and said that they had come from the Svatos family who had sheltered and helped parachutists in their small flat very near to Prague's Old Town Square. (One of the briefcases found at the scene also bore the stamp White Swan Hotel, Prague.) Curda admitted little else but the Gestapo soon realised that he knew more than he was letting on. After intense interrogation, some of it quite brutal, he began, in the words of the Gestapo, to *"sing like a canary"*.

He named Gabcik and Kubis but said he didn't know where they were hiding, which he genuinely didn't. He did, however, name the flat of the Moravec family as being crucial. Now the pieces started to fall in place for the Gestapo.

At around 5a.m. the next morning, the Gestapo stormed the flat of the Moravec family in Biscupova Street, a family flat that had provided a safe haven for the parachutists, Curda included.

Two ladies who lived in this same block of flats in 1942, Mrs Koprivova (lived in the flat above Moravecs) and Mrs Lancova (lived next door to Moravecs) both told me that this particular morning the street was full of soldiers. They said the Gestapo rang the bell to the flats and when the housekeeper, Mrs Spinkova, opened the door they pushed her out of the way and ran up to the second-floor flat. They told me that for a week after the raid, Gestapo officials stayed in the flat in the hope that someone from the Resistance would call, not knowing the family had been arrested.

Mrs Kristina Lancova, who was 12 at the time, remembered that prior to this, when "wanted posters" went up all over Prague showing Josef Valcik's photograph, her mum and sister were horrified as they recognised Valcik straight away as the man living in the Moravecs flat. They ran to the school of the 12 year old Kristina, to explain about the posters in case she said "I know him". The family never said a word. (The Gestapo were looking for Valcik from when he was working at the hotel in Pardubice. Valcik had heard word of this. That is why he went on the run to Prague)

As the police started the search, the family were made to stand facing the wall. They were all wearing their nightclothes. Mrs Moravec pleaded to go to the toilet. Eventually, they relented and while she was in the bathroom she took a poison capsule, which she usually kept behind a big cameo broach she wore.
With Mrs Moravec dead, her husband and young son looked on with horror. They were both taken away for "further questioning", with the young 21 year old son Ata (his real name was Vlastimil but everyone knew him as Ata) suffering the most incredibly brutal torture that one could ever imagine. He tried desperately to stay tight-lipped but when the Gestapo revived him with brandy and then took him into a room where they showed him his mother's head floating in a fish tank, young Ata broke down hysterically. He said he didn't know where the parachutists were but his mother always told him if he was ever in trouble, to seek refuge in the church of St Cyril in Resslova Street. (Mrs Lancova told me that she remembers young Ata wasn't actually there at the time of the arrest. She said he was staying with relatives in Pisek, which is about 150km away. She said the Gestapo sent him a telegram to "Come quick, father ill". She said he came and was duly arrested. However, given the time frame involved and most other accounts, I tend to believe that Ata was actually present at the time of the Gestapo raid.)

Last Stand

By 4.30 in the morning of June 18th, the whole area of the church of St Cyril was surrounded. The Germans had set up two rings of heavily armed steel. There could be no way out. Even the sewer system connected to the church was watched.

That very morning, three of the parachutists had chosen to stand guard, and sleep high up in the church choir loft. They were Jan Kubis, Adolf Opalka, and Jaroslav Svarc.

As Panwitz and his Gestapo entered the church, the three defenders were waiting. It's almost certain they must have heard all the commotion outside brought about by all the troops arriving. Because of the layout of the church, the parachutists had an excellent vantage point to fight, despite the fact that there was no means of escape. The only way of reaching the parachutists was through a narrow spiral staircase and even that had a locked gate on it.

Panwitz and his men first searched the Sacristan's small flat, which was on one side of the church. Then they entered the church proper, and as the search continued here, suddenly shots rang out. The battle had started.

Opposite the church, on the other side of the road, the SS had set up a machine-gun post and, on hearing the firing, immediately opened fire themselves, shooting out most of the windows of the church. This knee-jerk reaction proved dangerous and they were ordered to stop as they were also risking the lives of the Germans inside the church.

After initially backing out when the firing started, the Germans re-entered the church, this time led not by the Gestapo but by units of shock SS troops. They were armed to the teeth and led by Brigadefuhrer Karl von Treuenfeldt. Machine guns, grenades and pistols were used as the SS troops tried to work their way up the only access point, the narrow staircase. Meanwhile, the other four parachutists hiding in the crypt must have felt helpless, as they could hear the battle raging above them.

For nearly two hours, the three parachutists on the balcony defended their position, keeping at bay a whole detachment of crack SS troops. Time and again the SS tried to storm up the staircase but each time they were forced to retreat. Eventually, after two hours there was silence. Opalka and Svarc were dead, and Jan Kubis, who'd thrown the bomb at Heydrich, was gravely wounded, injuries that some say, mercifully, only kept him alive for a matter of minutes more. The German storm troopers had been under orders to try to capture the men alive but this had proved impossible. The bodies of the defenders were brought down and laid on the pavement outside, across the road from the church. Curda, the man who betrayed his fellow parachutists, was brought over to identify the bodies. After the two hour gun battle, the church interior was a mass of debris.

The men hiding in the crypt may have remained undiscovered but it's said that an extra set of clothing was discovered in the church. I feel sure that this, coupled with the fact that Curda must have said that none of the bodies belonged to Josef Gabcik, made the Gestapo search the church further. It is also said that the priest Father Petrek was forced to reveal that more men were hiding.

Panwitz called for plans of the layout of the church and it was then that an underground crypt was discovered. A further search of the church led to the discovery of a small trap door near to the main entrance of the church that had been used for access and supplies. As the trap door was lifted, a burst of gunfire rang out from below. Now another battle was on as the SS tried to find a way of reaching the men in their almost impregnable position.

At first, the Germans tried to lower volunteers down through the trap door with a rope tied to their waist. They were soon picked off by the defenders and so another way in had to be found. In the meantime Curda and the unfortunate Priest were brought in to try to appeal to the parachutists to surrender, but they were met by defiant cries of *"We are Czechs, we will never surrender"* followed by a burst of gunfire. It's also said that the young Ata Moravec was ordered to appeal to the men to give themselves up but he refused.

The Germans' attentions now turned to the ventilator grill that led from the crypt to the street outside. To give them access, the Germans knocked the grill in from the street, and this enabled them to throw in tear gas grenades. They were soon thrown out again. The Germans then brought big floodlights to shine in but these were smashed by gunfire from the defenders. Panwitz now sent for the local fire brigade. In the meantime, the defenders tried to dig their way out, by attacking the wall to find access to the sewers. Obviously the men were unaware that the sewer outlets were guarded but, in any event, the attempt was unsuccessful.

The fire brigade arrived. They were Czechs and were reluctant to help but they were forced to assist the Germans in the operation. They tried smoking the men out but the hoses were pushed out the same way they came in, through the ventilator grill. They then tried to flood the crypt but the parachutists managed to cut the hoses. Eventually, one fireman managed to grab a ladder that the defenders were using and pulled it out through the ventilator hole. Now the water hoses could continue unhindered, as without the ladder the parachutists couldn't reach the ventilator from their below-street level position.

The reluctant firemen try to flood the crypt

Outside in the street, Karl Frank paced up and down with anger. He wanted the men taken alive but the Germans were at a loss how to do this. Loudspeakers were brought and appeals made to the parachutists but again to no avail.

The Germans searched the whole church, pulling carpets back. They revealed a large marble slab in the floor, in front of the altar. This was the way used in the past for taking the coffins to the crypt. The Germans blew it apart. The slab broke in two and revealed an old stone staircase in to the crypt. With water pouring in from the ventilator shaft, and now a good access point for the SS, the defenders must have known that their time was up.

As the water rose to two and a half foot, four shots suddenly rang out from below. All four defenders, Josef Gabcik, Josef Valcik, Jan Hruby, and Josef Bublik, had taken their own lives with a pistol shot to the head.

An SS soldier warily went down the steps and then shouted back up *"Fertig"*, *("It's finished".)*

In the battle to take the church, the Germans had suffered fourteen fatalities and twenty one wounded. It's said that the Germans found eleven guns in the crypt but not one single round of ammunition remained. The men had saved their last bullets for themselves.

Aftermath

The bodies of the parachutists were taken away and formally identified. Their skulls were kept by the Gestapo, with the heads of Gabcik and Kubis being reported as being "kept in pickle jars" at Gestapo headquarters. After the war, they disappeared with some reports suggesting that the bones were being used many years later, by German medical students, for training purposes.

The Priest, the Bishop and other church officials were put on trial and shot in September of that year at the Kobylisy execution ground near Prague.

In an overseas publicity telegram issued by the British Ministry of Information to its representatives abroad on 28th May 1942, the day after the attack, it was stated that *'the Nazis do not overrate Heydrich's value. He has given them yeoman service ever since he joined the party.'* (UK National Archives HS4/39 323707)

After Heydrich's death the Germans launched a campaign called "Aktion Reinhard". This consisted of trainloads of people transported on special trains with Heydrich's name emblazoned on the front. The trains went straight to the killing grounds of Treblinka, Sobibor, and Belzec (concentration camps in the east, which were really extermination camps). Thousands lost their lives this way, to "commemorate" Heydrich.

252 members of the parachutists' family and friends, including people who had helped shelter them, or provided some other kind of assistance, were shot at Mathausen concentration camp on 24th October 1942. This group of people were known as "the parachutists group". It is said that the people were shot in the back of the head, at intervals of 2 minutes. To show how clinical the Germans were at the time, the Kubis family showed me some Death Certificates that the family received shortly after. These documents called Sterbeurkundes, were sent from Mauthausen and even show the exact time that the person perished. For instance Marie Kubisova died at 9.40am, and Jitka Kubisova perished at 10.32am

Jan Zelenka, cover name Hajsky, who had helped the men in many ways in his role as an important member of the resistance, ran to the bathroom and took a cyanide capsule when the Gestapo knocked on his door to arrest him. His son Milic also poisoned himself the same day, in a nearby park, when he realised the Gestapo were following him. Mrs Zelenkova was shot at Mauthausen camp on the 24th October 1942 as part of the murders of the so-called "parachute" group.

Karel Curda changed his identity to Karl Jerhot, took German citizenship, and continued to help the Gestapo with many of their enquiries, providing active help until the war ended. He collected much of the reward money, paid in instalments, and married a German girl. In the Anthropoid file at the UK National Archives in

Kew, there is a document dated 16th May 1945 in which there are other suspicions about Curda, from before the time of Anthropoid. The document, a letter from Lt-Cpl Strankmuller, who was the deputy head of Czech Military Intelligence based in the UK, states that on 8th May 1942, (Anthropoid was 27th May 1942) a man went to the Prague police and handed over a large sum of money, that he said he had been given to help him with his mission. It goes on to say that the man declared himself to be a parachutist and told of the hiding place of a hidden wireless transmitter set. The man had very similar false papers to Curda. The report says *"There is, therefore, a well-grounded suspicion that the unknown person could have been Curda."*

Kurt Daluege formally replaced Heydrich as Reich Protector and some of the Germans who took part in the police investigation, including von Panwitz and members of the SS, were rewarded with medals. It is said that 800 German soldiers and police took part in the battle for the church.

Lina Heydrich and Kurt Daluege arrive at a Memorial Service

Helena Vovsova told me that the clothes Heydrich was wearing on the day of the attack, including his bloodied white shirt, were placed in a glass display case near the main staircase at the Heydrich's villa, where they remained until near the end of the war. (Heider Heydrich, Heydrich's only surviving son, denied this happened, when I met him)

The church of St Cyril remained closed by order of the Nazis for the rest of the war.

Twelve months after the attack on Heydrich, a huge monument was put in place at the actual scene of the attack. It had a permanent SS guard of honour and featured a bust of Heydrich's head.

Karl Frank salutes the Heydrich Monument

A special Memorial Book was commissioned by Himmler in 1943 to commemorate the life of Heydrich, and recognising his dedication to the cause of National Socialism.

A Regiment of the Waffen SS on the Eastern front, the 6th SS Infantry Standarte (according to Himmler in his funeral oration) was renamed the Reinhard Heydrich Regiment, with its members being allowed to wear a cuff-title badge with the name Reinhard Heydrich embroided upon it.

Master and pupil.
Himmler (left) with Heydrich

Some later reports say that Lina had her husband's grave opened and the coffin dug up near the end of the war., or shortly afterwards. It's said that she had the coffin re-interred on the island of Fehmarn. However, I cannot see that this would have been logistically possible, with all the fighting and chaos going on in and around Berlin in early 1945. This cannot be taken too seriously until any evidence is brought to light in the future. When I met Heydrichs daughter Marte, she said that it wouldn't have been possible to move the body, as did Heider Heydrich, and I have to agree. To the best of my knowledge, the grave is still undisturbed. Until recently I believed the most likely location was near the middle of Plot A of the Invaliden Cemetery. However, new evidence has come to light to me which, in fact, points to the grave being in Plot D of the cemetery, which is the first field on the left of the entrance, with the grave being quite near to the cemetery entrance. The cemetery authorities informed me that all burial records were lost in a fire as a result of the Allied bombing of Berlin during World War 2, and to add further complications to research, the cemetery is located where there was part of the divide of east and west Berlin, and as a result some of the cemetery was altered.

The attack on Heydrich cost thousands of Czech lives, and some still argue that the price paid for what was achieved was way too high. However, it was the main direct action of Czech resistance to the German occupiers and it put the nation back on the world map when its importance was slipping. Shortly afterwards, the Allies declared the Munich Agreement was null and void and vowed to restore the Czech nation back to its pre-1938 borders at the end of the war. At the war's end, Benes returned to Prague as President, still denying knowledge of Anthropoid, he said, *"until it was too late"*.

At the end of the war, when the Czechs finally rose up against the Germans, Karel Curda was put on trial. At the end of the trial Curda was asked by the Judge how he could have betrayed his friends, and country. Curda replied *"I think you would do the same for one million marks."* He was hanged at Prague's Pankrac Prison on 29th April 1947.

The same fate befell Karl Hermann Frank who was hanged on 22nd May 1946, and Heydrich's successor Kurt Daluege, already a very ill man, who was hanged on 24th October 1946. Frank's hanging took place in front of an invited audience, which included some surviving mothers of Lidice.

The Prague monument to Heydrich was torn down at the end of the war.

Lorna's Story-Part Two

The Last Will and Testaments of Josef Gabcik and Jan Kubis, written on 28th December 1941, clearly states that should anything happen to the men, they wanted the relevant authorities to inform Lorna and Edna Ellison. The men died on the 18th June 1942, and yet the telegram in this book clearly shows that the Ellison family weren't "officially" informed until 3rd August 1945. Whilst this can be largely excused, considering there was a war on, I still feel that given the men's devotion to duty and the consequences for the Czechoslovak nation that followed, an injustice or an oversight to the men's wishes had taken place. Were the authorities waiting for confirmation of their deaths?

The Ellison family actually heard about the heroic deaths of their two "Czech friends" (as the family called them) from neighbours, after it had appeared in a newspaper in the summer of 1942. There was a gap of three years between the family hearing about the deaths and being "officially" informed.

For political reasons some of the important decision makers had tried to distance themselves from the high cost of Anthropoid. Politics aside, however, the Ellison family was a big part of Jan and Josef's time spent in Britain and clearly held a place in the men's hearts.

When I met Lorna Ellison, she told me that she always wanted to visit Prague, as the men had wished her to do so. (See Lorna's story) I decided there and then to try to make this possible for Lorna in order to honour the bravery and sacrifices made by those involved and the sacrifices made, not just by the parachutists and their families but also the other brave men and women who helped make Operation Anthropoid a success in its mission. Albeit 64 years later, I was determined to take Lorna Ellison to Prague.

It was far from easy to achieve. Thankfully, a British newspaper 'The Mail on Sunday' came to the rescue, as quite honestly, I was running out of options to make the visit possible. One of the first things I did, once I had spoken at length to Lorna, was to make an appointment to visit the Czech Ambassador in London, who was delighted to hear that I had found Lorna, and was pleased to be able to invite her for tea. To keep the appointment time of 2pm, I had left my house at 7am that morning but on arrival at the Embassy the Ambassador told us that he was extremely busy and had an urgent appointment he had to keep! In the very short time that we had together, he was kind to Lorna for which I will always be grateful but I came away in the knowledge that a visit had not been arranged and in fact we were a long way away. However, the day was not wasted as I was able to take Lorna the short distance to show her the actual place in London where her friends had had their last photographs taken before being flown out of Britain.

Many of my letters and enquiries to official bodies either went unanswered, or worse were met by negative responses. Perhaps I was getting mixed up in something with political implications but surely this should have been above all that? Some either wouldn't, or couldn't help and others were immediately concerned about any financial cost a visit may incur. Whilst I fully understood that I was asking the Czech Government to effectively cover the cost of flights and hotels for the trip and that officials were accountable for all items of expenditure, I felt, and still feel, that this small cost could be justified as money well-spent. The Ellison family had looked after Jan Kubis and Josef Gabcik, when quite honestly, they had very little themselves. What they had, however, they shared completely with the two soldiers.

Eventually *The Mail on Sunday*, in return for coverage of the story, agreed to cover the cost of making such a visit possible.

I was very fortunate to be put in contact with the Czech Legion, a marvellous veteran's organisation, which in turn put me in contact with a retired Colonel of the Czech Parachute Regiment, a man named Frantisek Veis. Colonel Veis proved to be a man of total integrity and one who strongly believed in justice. He was a man who had been imprisoned under Communist rule for 10 years (guilty of so-called political activities like trying to leave the country!). He worked tirelessly and devotedly in making the proposed visit happen. He was, and is, a credit to the uniform of a Czech paratrooper and I believe Jan and Josef would have been proud of him.

Right from the start, Colonel Veis treated the whole proposed visit like a military operation. He compiled lists and plans and accompanied me as an advisor, interpreter, guide and friend. (He has also continued to do so, whilst I have been writing this book, accompanying me on several trips around the Czech Republic even letting me stay in his house while I did my research.) Quite simply, Lorna's visit would not have happened without Colonel Veis. That is how important he has been.

I met another man, at a Memorial Service in Prague, who helped me enormously. His name is Pavel Bem and he is the Mayor of Prague. This is a good man. When I found doors not being opened to me, sometimes by officials in his offices, I literally walked up to the Mayor when I saw him at a ceremony in Prague and asked him to help. I told him that I had heard he was "a man who believed in justice". He said that he was and listened to me explaining some of the difficulties I was experiencing, the frustrations I was feeling and what I was trying to do. I can state quite categorically that this is clearly a man of whom the city of Prague can feel proud of. He wrote to me personally, got his staff involved, extended the hospitality of the Mayor's Residence for the duration of the trip and, in short, put the full weight of his office behind the trip.

Eventually, the pieces started to fall in to place and, with the help of the Czech Military Attaché based in London, Colonel Petr Miller, I was able to put together an itinerary for Lorna's visit. Colonel Miller even went so far as to provide us with Ministry of Defence transport for the duration.

Thanks to a number of people, Lorna was going to get the VIP treatment and her trip was going to be a memorable one. Starting with a couple of employees of Manchester Airport, Maria Whelan and Derrick Heatley, Lorna got the royal treatment.

I'd tried to set the itinerary so that we travelled almost in the same order that Jan and Josef had. Our first stop then, was to Nehvizdy, where the local Mayor was there to greet us along with other town officials and even some survivors of the time of the parachutists landing in December 1941. Lorna was able to lay flowers at a memorial stone to Anthropoid. She did a couple of television interviews and it seemed most of this small village had come out to meet us.

We reluctantly had to leave the warm hospitality of Nehvidzy behind, as we had an itinerary to keep, and only a relatively short time. We moved on to Panenske Brezany, the home of Heydrich during his time in Prague. This is a place that has never really been open to the public but, with the full weight of officialdom behind us now, we were driven through the main gates. This place was a big part of the Heydrich story and we were able to get Lorna full access, showing her inside and outside of the villa. I spent time showing Lorna the gates that Heydrich had been driven out of on that fateful day.

From there, we followed the route Heydrich had taken, showing Lorna the places that Jan and Josef had hidden while formulating a pattern to Heydrich's movements and the area, near a small copse of trees, where the two men considered attacking the car.

We ended the day at the historic bend in the road where the attack took place. I showed Lorna the approximate places that Jan and Josef had been standing. We then followed the escape route of Josef Gabcik, whilst he was being chased by the chauffeur. Lorna was absolutely delighted to see nearby roads named after her friends.

By this time Lorna was tired, and I knew that tomorrow was a big day, so we retired to get some rest. We had managed to cram a lot in to our first day. Next day, Sunday, was the anniversary service of the battle in the church of St Cyril.

Sunday 18th June was a special day. We went to the church of St Cyril and St Methodius, and while a band played, we were invited to take part in the parade. In honour of her friends' memories, Lorna refused her usual wheelchair and demanded to walk in the parade. Whilst she held on strongly to my arm, we walked to the ventilator shaft with its memorial plaque and laid some flowers to honour the men. The Prime Minister of the Czech Republic was there alongside many veterans. We spoke at length to the British Ambassador and her Military Attaché before going inside for the truly beautiful memorial service, with front row chairs reserved for us. With all these dignitaries present the good people of Prague still found time to make Lorna the guest of honour.

From there, we were whisked to another outdoor Remembrance Service, this time to honour all the parachutists and once again front row seats were reserved for Lorna, where we were able to sit and watch as some of today's parachutists landed. A real highlight of the day came when we were introduced to a gentleman by the name of Jiri Dusik, the nephew of Jan Kubis.

Next day, we were given a full private tour of the church of St Cyril and its crypt by the Dean of the church Dr Suvarsky and his wife. Dr Suvarsky had conducted the service the day before in his official capacity. I have always found him to be a very obliging and affable man. He is an absolute credit to the history of the church and the people who gave their lives for sheltering the parachutists. Being in the crypt was a very emotional time for Lorna. She was so proud of her friends.

Then it was on to look at the "safe houses" used by the men. I particularly wanted Lorna to see these because without such help, Operation Anthropoid could not have functioned.

From there we went to lay flowers at the Kobylisy execution grounds. This piece of land, where so many people lost their lives, is now a very poignant memorial place, with names of the people who were executed there, written on a huge plaque.

The night was rounded off with a terrific meal held in Lorna's honour at a Prague hotel, The Hotel Duo. The owner of this hotel is a man called Josef Horal. This proud ex-serviceman does so much unsung work for veterans, entertaining many visitors from British Legions.

On Tuesday, our last day, we attended a reception at the Slovak Embassy in Prague. Josef Gabcik was Slovak and the people there were so proud showing us photographs of a Regiment of the Slovakian Army now named after him.

Our last port of call was to a cemetery in Dablice and, in particular, a small piece of unmarked grass. Recent reports suggest that here the parachutists were put in an unmarked grave. Lorna laid flowers here and spent some time with her own thoughts and memories.

There was only time to say our goodbyes, as we had to catch the plane home. The whole trip had been exhausting both emotionally and physically for Lorna. Her health hadn't been great before the trip but it is a journey that I know she wouldn't have missed for the world. Lorna was so proud of her friends Jan and Josef. She thought it terrific that people remember them today.

For me, it was a proud time having been able to organize the trip for Lorna Ellison to see Prague and the places connected to Jan Kubis and Josef Gabcik. It was a trip that was long overdue.

Heider Heydrich

I had heard so many horror stories about people who had been given short shrift by him, that it was with a great deal of trepidation that I flew to Munich to meet Heider Heydrich, the only living son, and the family spokesperson on the life of Reinhard Heydrich. (Though he hadn't previously done much talking!) Even my emails prior to my visit were returned with short answers and what I perceived as a great deal of suspicion. I was feeling the effects of a heavy cold and was really unsure how this meeting would go.

From the moment I met him at Munich airport, he was totally charming. Showing true hospitality, we went to his house where a meal was waiting. Heider had clearly suffered in his life because of his surname. The stories he told me about some of the episodes with journalists made me cringe.

There is absolutely no way whatsoever that he can be responsible for anything done by, or in, his father's name. Yet Heider and his other siblings have carried the burden of their father's infamy throughout their lives. It is something that has always been bubbling under the surface of Heider's life and yet he has grown up to be a fine and successful man, with a lovely family of his own. He and his wife have been together since they were very young.

Why, after some 66 years, had I been the one he had chosen to speak to about his father? Maybe my charm, my wisdom, my wit? Seriously, I don't know why. I had spent a great deal of effort to gain his trust prior to my visit. He knew my knowledge of the subject matter and I think also I had made him aware that I was trying to write a factual account, and not relying on wildly speculative theories. He knew, because I had told him, that I had travelled extensively researching Anthropoid and perhaps all this had an affect. Or, he may have just felt he was now at the time of his life to discuss these things. I may have been in the right place, at the right time. Even if this was the case, I knew he had to trust me, to know that I was genuine in trying to find the truth.

My first meeting with Heider was slightly nervous for both of us. I tried to ease him along with questions relating to facts that have always caused disagreements with Heydrich researchers. Was his father right-handed or left-handed I asked? Heider wasn't aware that researchers had discussed such things and was surprised that such questions are debated on internet chat rooms. We have seen many pictures of him fencing or writing right-handed but some put up the theories that the photographs are, in fact, negatives so it is all reversed. So, many theories circulated, without there being definitive answers. I also wanted to have a more complete picture and understanding of Reinhard Heydrich. Perhaps only people who are so wrapped up in a subject, like I am with Anthropoid, can understand the wanting-to-know such trivial details. Heider looked me in the eye and stated "Categorically, 100%, my father was right-handed". He explained how his father sword-fenced, played the violin, played the piano, played tennis, and wrote right-handed. No mistake. I almost jumped for joy at this, as we had pondered the question for years! I realise how incredibly sad that this must sound to you the reader, but to me….wow! Heider and I laughed at this, at my excitement in knowing for definite the answer to this question. I now feel that this helped break the ice between us. We got on famously after that.

Heider explained how he was only 8 years old at the time of Anthropoid. Previously to this, his father was always busy, often leaving the house in the morning and not returning home until late at night. Either that or he was away in France, Norway, Holland, Germany or could be in any other occupied country. His special memories of his father and time spent with him are really confined only to when they went on holiday skiing or summer holidays on Fehmarn Island.

Talking to Heider made me realise that of all the bad things written and reported about Reinhard Heydrich, (and they are countless), to these people he was a father and a husband. He was simply "Papa" to his children. However, we always have to be aware that Europe was in turmoil when Reinhard Heydrich was growing up. Many people in Germany were blaming Jewish influence for the poverty and the collapse of the German currency. It was even blamed for losing the First World War. Such thinking wasn't confined to Reinhard Heydrich. It was a common belief of a large proportion of the population. They blamed Jewish bankers and industrialists for speculating in the economy. Whilst this is in no way an apology for Reinhard Heydrich, Heider was at pains to explain that his father had grown up in these times and been greatly influenced by it. "My father", said Heider,"was an idealist who had been caught up and swept along with the politics of the day". Heider, a clever and thinking man, whilst naturally trying to protect his father somewhat, explained that his father was an intelligent and very capable man, who would have been successful in most things he had attempted. I can associate with that. "However", explained Heider, "Papa grew up in an era of turmoil, with economic, racial and political conflict all around. I believe it was kismet or fate that Papa was born in an era when the line of thinking was how it was then."

I don't believe Heider is offering excuses, or living in denial. Rather, he is just trying to tell it how it was and what he believes. Certainly Obergruppenfuhrer Heydrich seems to have been head and shoulders above most of the top echelon of Nazi party hierarchy, in both ability and intelligence. Does that make his crimes worse because others might be excused for not knowing any better? Well, I think that's a question for people to decide for themselves.

Heider went on to explain that he doesn't feel guilty because of his name. He does, however, feel the shame of his nation. He rightly said that he would only feel guilty if he had actually done something wrong personally. He asked "What have I done, only to be German?" He said "I was born German and born a Heydrich. I cannot change it even if I wanted to, so is that enough reason to feel guilty? I have some very close friends who are Jewish. They know who my father was but they are, thankfully, still my friends. I have visited concentration camps to pay my respects as a human being."

"As a family we have suffered, and had to live with the strain" he explained. "After the war, my mother had no money and we children had little food. We all had to live with my grandparents. It was only some years later that my mother was able to receive a small pension from the German Government for the death in action of my father. I have never spoken about my father before now. You are the first writer I have ever agreed to see. Even now I am concerned that you may write a distortion of what I really want to say. I have every respect for historians but I have always believed that anything I say will be used against my family. That's the reason I haven't spoken about my father until now. Nothing I say can change things. My friends know that I totally disagree with what happened in the concentration camps. So, from an early age, I decided the best thing to do for my sanity was to only look forward and not back. I've not involved my children. I have only tried to be a good father and husband. We have four great children, one of whom is a doctor. I have encouraged them, tried to set a good example to them and sent them out in the world."

Without any attempt to dilute his father's deeds, he pointed out to me, historically correctly, that so much was blamed on Heydrich during the trials of top Nazis, which took place after the war in Nuremburg. Heider believes this was a pre-agreed plan of action prior to the trial in order to shift blame, and any responsibility for crimes, on to a man who was dead and so couldn't answer back. Adolph Eichmann, who ran the department of the Gestapo that dealt with Jewish affairs, Department 1V, also blamed Heydrich for most things, after he was captured by the Israelis in Argentina. He was put on trial in Jerusalem. (Eichmann was eventually found guilty and was hanged in 1962)

The Heydrich family have few, if any, possessions or even photographs from the time spent with their father. "Most of the documents and photographs my mother either had to sell, or lent to journalists and never had them returned. Most of the photographs the family have now are from published books that anyone can get. I have many books written about my father. Some of the books are even in languages such as French that I can't read. I purchased them anyway."

"My father wasn't anti-Czech. He was only working for the good of Germany, and I believe at the time many Czechs respected that. He punished Czechs and Germans alike. Some Germans were also executed for corruption, black market practices, racketeering and the like. This can be proved. My mother also told me categorically that when my father lay dying in hospital, he didn't want any retribution or revenge. He knew that the attack was from outsiders and only wanted the guilty ones hunted down. He also worried that anything different from this would harm production in the factories. My mother went to the hospital on a daily basis and stayed all of the time but we children never went. I have read in books that Himmler was worried that my father had become too powerful, and wanted him out of the way. I believe this is complete rubbish. My father's wound was infected and even the best doctors didn't know how to treat it. Himmler would not, or could not, have made medical decisions without my mother's knowledge. My mother was always at the bedside and she was consulted in every medical decision. She was pregnant at the time and, with all the worries of my father's health, our family were not kept up to date with the Gestapo investigation to find the parachutists. Lidice happened without our knowledge. Possibly it could have been done because the leaders were so scared and vulnerable to attack. They wanted a warning to be made, to protect them in the future and hopefully to deter would-be attackers. Lidice was most definitely not done with my father's, or our family's, blessing." It is certainly historically correct that many of the atrocities carried out by the Nazis in the Czech lands happened after Heydrichs death.

"There are many things written in books about my father that just aren't true", he said. "Papa played the violin. But it is never written that he played the piano to a high standard. I don't believe stories that my father once placed the Crown of St Wenceslas on his head and this led to a curse costing him and my brother their lives. My mother also said this simply did not happen. (This is often reported to have happened shortly after Heydrich took over in Prague, at a ceremony when he was given for "safekeeping" some of the sacred keys to the city. Its said he saw the crown and placed it on his head, something which locals believed would carry a curse on anyone not entitled to wear the crown)

Admiral Canaris was a true friend of my father when we lived in Berlin. I remember we used to play with his children. (Canaris was in charge of the Abwehr, the German Military Intelligence. There was much speculation and suspicion about him being a double-agent, and of there being friction between him and Heydrich. Canaris was executed by the Germans shortly before the end of the war)

There is also no truth in the rumour that my father had Jewish ancestry, none whatsoever.

It is not true that my father's body was removed from the cemetery in Berlin. In early 1945 when it was supposed to have happened, we had other problems to deal with. It couldn't have happened. I visited my father's grave only recently and, although it is unmarked, I know where it is. It is in the same place as it has always been. It has been reported that our family renounced all claim on the grave to a Berlin Professor in 2001. Any such claim would have come via me and I have had no such enquiry.

I have seen many photographs of my father's funeral but I have little memory of it now. I can't recall what Hitler said to me. My biggest memory of it is the amount of people who were there, and all the flowers. My brother Klaus and I were in the front row. To us it was just a big spectacle."

A very rare family photograph of a young Heider (left) with his mother Lina, brother Klaus, and a young baby sister Silke

"My brother Klaus and I were very close, almost like twins. Remember, we didn't even go out to school where we may have met other children. Our teacher, Trude Schilling, came to the house. When Klaus died in 1943, it had a much bigger impact on me than my father's death. Klaus was riding his bike and I was hanging on to the back of it, when the truck crashed in to us, just outside the gates of our home. Klaus was killed but I was uninjured. Klaus was buried in the grounds of Panenske Brezany and I am convinced he still rests there. It was claimed that he was disinterred when we left Prague and his body taken with us. Again this isn't true. I can remember the day we left for good. I rode my bicycle around the grounds one last time and his grave was undisturbed. My sisters and I have tried to visit his grave but, each time we have gone, it has not proved possible to get access. It is a dear wish of mine to visit my brother's grave to lay flowers. I believe I would know where his grave was even if the layout of the grounds had changed over the years. However, for political reasons, I don't believe we will ever be granted permission.

I visited Prague to see where we used to live for part of my life. People shouldn't look at this in any sinister way. I am just a human being and I think it is quite usual for people, as they get older, to want to see places connected to their life. I visited Hradcany Castle where we first lived when the family came to Prague. I also visited the crypt in St Cyril's. I tried to find the scene of the attack on my father but I couldn't locate it. I went to the outside of Panenske Brezany. This house holds many happy memories of my childhood, even though family tragedies happened there. The staff were very friendly to us children when we lived there and we also went outside the grounds to play with the local gamekeeper's children. I can remember my father's military assistant was a man by the name of Klukon. I think my father smoked cigars because one time my brother and I went in to his office there was a box of them on his desk. We thought they were edible so we ate some and we were very ill afterwards. These are things I remember, not military matters."

(In 2008 I was able to make the desired visit happen for Heider. We met in Prague and I was able to take him to all the places he wished to see, with full access. He arrived with his wife, daughter and granddaughter and so 3 generations of Heydrich's family were present. It was clearly an emotional time for Heider, reliving his childhood and almost sprinting around the places. I was able to explain to him about the places relevant to the attack, and also show him the new monument that has been placed near the scene of the attack on his father. Heider in no way, shape, or form can bear any responsibility for the events that happened when he was a very young boy.)

On The Trail of Anthropoid

This chapter is only intended as a guide for anyone visiting Prague and wishing to see some of the places connected to Operation Anthropoid. I would always do some homework before going to Prague and I've found the Prague Tourist Board in London more helpful than the tourist offices in the City itself.

Some of the places like Lidice, Nehvidzy, Lezaky and Panenske Brezany are quite a way outside the city and so I've not included them in this chapter. To visit these places you would probably need to hire a car, or maybe organise a special tour.

Prague itself is a beautiful city and is fast emerging as one of the most popular weekend breaks for European people. It's a two hour flight from Britain and many budget airlines now visit it. When I first went in the early 1990s, the price of the flights was more expensive than now, over fourteen years later! The airport of Prague, Ruzyne, is about a half hour drive from the city. Taxis are always available, as is public transport.

The people are very hospitable, and the standard of hotel and restaurants is comparable with most European cities. I've watched as Prague has emerged from its former communist past and now, every time I visit, I see change, not least in the price of goods and services that have risen considerably since my first visit. It can be very cold in the winter but, whatever the season, it is still a stunning city.

As with any major city, common sense when travelling is essential, being aware of pickpockets and over-priced taxis. It has been rumoured that the current Mayor of Prague, Pavel Bem, has been known to actually travel in disguise using the city's taxis and restaurants to try to stamp out over-pricing for tourists! Whenever converting money to the Czech Crown, only ever use official booths. A common scam is when people approach you in the street to offer a better rate of exchange, only for you to later find that what you have actually exchanged to is some other country's currency worth an awful lot less than the Czech Crown! Beware!

Because of the rapid development of Prague, the information contained here is only intended as a guide and is only correct at the time of going to print. I know plans are in place to expand the public transport system with new stops being added. If in doubt though, I've always found that when asking a local about the location of a place, the term "Atentat" is well-known. (Atentat is German for Assassination) Say 'Anthropoid' and you will get some strange looks.

The public transport system in Prague is superb. It is a great idea to buy a 24 hour travel pass or even a three-day one as these offer unlimited travel on the public system. If you do buy a pass make sure you stamp your ticket in the machines the first time you use it. Bus and tram services are excellent in Prague. I find, however, that the best way to travel around is by using the underground train system. It really is a fantastic service. It's new, modern, cheap and very efficient. It is also colour and letter co-ordinated and so it is very easy to use once you get your head around it. The colours used are green, yellow and red. Green is A, yellow is B, and red is C. Maps are readily available. I've spent some of my happiest times criss-crossing the city, hopping off a tram to get the train or bus in pursuit of Anthropoid-related places.

I have not dealt with the sites of Anthropoid in any particular order here. Rather, I have tried to group them together in closeness of locations to each other. If my itinerary is not suitable to meet your needs, plan your own trip in the order of priority you wish to see places.

Hradcany Castle, which was Heydrich's main office during his time in Prague, and also his destination on the fateful day, is a big complex, with beautiful gardens. I would always allow half a day to see this. The easiest way to the castle is to use the tram from the city centre. This takes you to the castle gates, saving the walk uphill. If using the Metro, take the metro line A (Green) and there are two stops you could use, either Hradcanska or Malostranska. Whichever one you use there is then a fifteen minute hike to the castle. From the metro station, there are plenty of brown signs showing the visitor the direction to take. The main changing-of-the-guard at the castle now takes place at twelve noon.

Many Nazi dignitaries visited the Castle during the occupation. These included Hitler, Himmler, Funk and Speer. (Many of the Nazi top brass were known as Golden Pheasants due to the outlandish and decorative uniforms they wore!)

Hitler's architect Dr. Speer (left) is shown around Prague

The first courtyard is where many troops were reviewed by Heydrich and Himmler. It is also the place where Heydrich's coffin was laid in state just after he died. Under the big decorative stone arch, the Matthias Gate, the Germans hung a huge wooden copy of an Iron Cross, with Heydrich's body placed in front of it, surrounded by guards and 6 eternal flames. Tens of thousands thronged through the gates to pass the coffin, many doing so out of fear rather than respect.

Walk under the Matthias Gate, and look to the right. There you will see a staircase which is not accessible. These are the steps leading to the Spanish Hall and one of the most famous photographs of Heydrich was taken as he walked up these steps with Himmler and Karl Frank.

In the vicinity of Hradcany Castle is the Wallenstien Palace, where Heydrich attended a special concert of his father's music on the night before he was attacked.

After visiting the castle take the metro line A (green) in the direction of the town and alight at the station marked Mustek. This is the nearest stop for Old Town Square, one of the nicest places in Prague. Find the Astronomical Clock and stand with your back to it. Now, slightly to the right but straight on you will see a passageway under a high arch. This is called Melantrichova. Go along this passage, past the shops and keep going until it turns left. In the corner on the right is an arched doorway marked number 15. In this courtyard was the home of the Svatos family. The actual flat used, number 10, was on the top floor with the windows overlooking the main street. If you go through to the courtyard using the doorway where the plaque to the family is on the right, the family flat will be at this end. This was one of the regular "safehouses" used by the parachutists. Josef Gabcik had borrowed a briefcase from the family to hide his machine gun in and it was this very briefcase that the traitor Karel Curda identified at Gestapo headquarters from the repair stitching that had been done by Mrs Svatos. All the Svatos family paid with their lives and there is a plaque in the courtyard honouring them, which roughly translates as *The Svatos family were helpful to the Freedom Fighters. They fell but the Czech nation remembers them. They all died at Mauthausen.*

From here, it's only a short walk to the bottom of Wenceslas Square. As you face the top, over on your right you will see a Bata shoe shop at number 6 Wenceslas Square. In 1942 it was also a Bata shoe shop. In the window to the right of the doorway was where the Gestapo displayed items found at the scene of the attack such as Josef's bicycle and beige raincoat along with a sign asking if anyone knew who they belonged to and details of the massive reward on offer for information. Just off Wenceslas Square near here in a street called Stepanska Street, is the Hotel Alcron. This fine hotel, which opened in 1932, was were many Nazi dignitaries were entertained during Heydrich's tenure in Prague.

At the top of Wenceslas Square, which can be reached directly using metro station Muzeum on either A or C (green or red), you will find a McDonalds on the corner. Turn left here, going down a road called Washingtonova. Here you will find a hotel called Hotel Esplanade. This terrific hotel, which dates from 1927, is where Heydrich stayed the first night he arrived in Prague to assume office. Just a couple of yards away, on the corner is the Petschek Palace, home of the Prague Gestapo. The actual street it is in is called Politickych Veznu. On the corner of the building is a black plaque signifying the building's sinister past. (The plaque translates roughly as: *This building housed the terrible prisons of the Gestapo. There was fighting, suffering and dying for the freedom of our Motherland. We will never forget the memory and dedication of their deaths, and we will keep the memory of their mission forever. People watch out!*)

The Gestapo building is the dark grey one with pillars on the doorway. It's now the Czech Ministry of Foreign Trade and, as such, is obviously not open to the public, apart from the appointment-only museum in the basement. It is a shame that the building itself is not open to the public, as it has amazing wooden panelling in the corridors and is a magnificent building inside. The basement museum itself is run by the Czech Freedom Fighters Association.

In the basement museum there are 11 cells which the Gestapo used for "special cases" and also the room where the prisoners had to wait to be questioned. It is sarcastically termed the "cinema", due to the prisoners having to wait in rows, not being allowed to speak and only stare at the blank wall ahead. After a period of time prisoners were imagining things projected on the wall, like a cinema. The original benches where the people sat and waited are still there. Altogether, during the Nazi occupation, 35,721 people were questioned by the Gestapo in Petschek Palace.

In front of the cells is a dark area which often has flowers on it, along with a Czech flag. This was actually the site of a staircase down which coffins were transported straight out to the inner courtyard, to save taking them through any public view. This inner courtyard is not accessible to the general public, and anyway it is largely changed from its 1942 description. It is now partly used as a car park for deliveries.

The Gestapo employed between 600 and 1000 people in this building. Through the main doorway came the traitor Karel Curda to volunteer the information he had.

I spoke to a survivor of Petschek Palace, a lady by the name of Libuse Nachtmannova, who, by her own admission, is one of the lucky ones to be still alive. She told me about how the system worked, when she was taken prisoner, as a 21 year old, in 1941. Her crime had been to help people move addresses when they were on the run from the Gestapo. At the time she was a member of the National Defence, an underground resistance movement. She was held in nearby Pankrac Prison for 3 months and was brought a number of times to Petschek Palace for questioning before she was finally placed in Raavensbruck concentration camp for 4 years. She said that when they were brought to the "cinema" room, they had to sit there and wait. They couldn't move or talk as there were guards present. Then they would finally call your name and you had to jump to attention and go straight out the side door to be questioned.

From Petschek Palace, return to the underground metro and take the red line (C). Five stops later alight at Kobylisy. From here it's quite a hike of maybe a mile, (and even then not easy to find) to the former Kobylisy execution grounds which has now been turned in to a fitting memorial. I always take a taxi from the metro station as it's not expensive and there is a taxi rank outside the metro station. Alternatively, you can take the trams numbered 17 and 25, or the bus numbers 175 or 200. The Memorial itself is set in a park inside a housing estate. When you arrive here, have a look at the dates of the people on the memorials and see how many were close to 27 May 1942, the date of the attack on Heydrich. The officials from St Cyril's Church were amongst those executed here.

If you do take my advice and use a taxi from the metro station, ask the driver to wait for you at the Memorial as it won't be easy to get a taxi to return from here. Then return to the Kobylisy metro station (or if not going to the execution grounds, take the metro to Kobylisy anyway). From the Kobylisy metro station it's about a 10 minute walk along a road called Zenklova, to the scene of the attack on Heydrich.

Zenklova in the Liben district of Prague 8 was called Kirchmeyer Strasse in 1942 but it is the same street that Heydrich was chauffeur-driven on the fateful day. I like to walk along this road as it seems largely unchanged from what it must have looked like to Heydrich in the passenger seat.

Walk along Zenklova and keep going until you get to the main intersection. This is the remodelled bend very near to where the actual attack took place. You will know you are here as it's the only place with a big pedestrian underpass close by. The old electric station over the road can clearly be seen in original Gestapo photographs of Heydrich's damaged car.

 Despite some historical authors saying there is a plaque on the underpass, don't go looking as there isn't one! The actual small plaque is found by retracing your steps around the famous bend and taking a sharp left through the hedge. On a wall there, near to the bus stop, is the small plaque. There is talk and plans to erect a significant plaque to commemorate Anthropoid, but at the time of writing, this is the only plaque in the vicinity. There is a new stone memorial very near by as well, close to the bus stop, which it is hoped to be the cornerstone of a bigger planned memorial.

From the bend (or plaque) walk a few steps in the direction you arrived. The first left turn is now called Gabcikova, named after Josef Gabcik, who ran down this street being chased by the chauffeur. You really are in the thick of the action now.

Walk down this road. At the crossroads Josef ran straight on. At this point just pause and look to the road on the right. This is called Kubisova, named after Jan Kubis.

Keep going straight down. Were there shots fired on this road, or had the chauffeur jammed his gun as described in an earlier chapter? Was it Josef firing his pistol? Bystanders and sunbathers heard shots. Was this the Resistance shooting at the chauffeur to try to help Josef? Perhaps we'll never know.

Josef got to the next junction and turning slightly to his left ran across the road. In 1942 the Brauners Butcher Shop was located here and Josef ran in to try to escape out of the back. Brauners was down a couple of steps, next door to the doorway now numbered 1153, almost directly behind the concrete enclosure currently used for the rubbish bins. There are small oblong windows now (used as a boiler room today) but, at the time, this was the location of the butcher's doorway.

Josef ran out again and, after shooting the chauffeur here at the doorway, turned right and ran towards the main road again. This street is now named Valcikova (after Josef Valcik). Josef Gabcik made good his escape, apparently through some nearby gardens.

From here I would suggest taking a bus to the metro station. When you get on to the metro system, you need to be on the orange line (B). Exit at the station called Karlovo Namesti. Take the left hand exit from the underground tube station and this will bring you out at Resslova Street. Turn left at the exit and there is the Czechoslovak Orthodox Church of St Cyril and Methodius.

The church itself is rarely open to the public except when there is a service taking place. The outer main doors are, however, usually open and a glass domed-shaped panel has been fitted so you can look in to the church. If so, look to your left and you will clearly see the small wooden staircase, which is usually locked with a metal gate, as it was the morning the Gestapo and SS arrived. This provided the only access up in to the choir loft, almost above your head. Up above, you will see the high balcony of the church. This is where three parachutists fought and died. (Jan Kubis was taken away unconscious and died soon after)

If you look on the floor, almost in to the left hand corner, you can just make out the trap door that was the main access used to the crypt. This was where Karel Curda and others were brought in to try to talk the men out. In front of the altar, under the carpet, is the bigger access point that the Germans eventually found and blew up to reveal the stairs.

The crypt is usually open and is now a museum. This is a must-see part of any Anthropoid related trip. It's a poignant place which has remained unchanged since the men were hidden there. Outside, the ventilator grill has a plaque above it which says *"In this Orthodox Church St Cyril and Methodius National Heroes from the Czechoslovak Foreign Army died for our freedom on 18/6/1942"*. Then it lists the names of the people who gave their lives and goes on to say *"And the other Czech Patriots who were hiding the parachutists and were executed. Eternal Memory"*.

Across the road from the plaque on the corner of Resslova Street and Vaclavska was where they laid the bodies of the dead parachutists out for identification.

Biscupova Street, in the Zizkov district of Prague, is an important part of the Anthropoid story. In this street lived the Moravec family who did so much to help hide the parachutists. Across the same street was the home of Jan Zelenka the underground man who also gave massive help to Anthropoid. Both houses are marked by plaques signifying the famous occupants. Biscupova Street can be reached by taking the metro to the station called Florence on lines A or C (red or orange). From there take a bus numbered 133 and this stops right by the Moravec's apartment. Zelenka's house is now number 4 Biscupova Street. The actual flat is number 7 on the first floor. From street level, the window of this flat is to the right of the doorway and, at the time of writing, directly above a small clothes shop. The current occupiers of the flat were glad to show me around. They even showed me the small bathroom to which Jan Zelenka ran when the Gestapo arrived, and where he took his own life. The current occupiers of the flat, Mr and Mrs Cmiral, explained to me that the bathroom had white tiled walls at the time and, when they moved in, there were bullet marks on the wall.

The Moravec family flat was a vital part of the parachutists hiding from the police before, and immediately after, Anthropoid. It was where Josef Valcik lived for much of his time on the run. The Moravec flat is at number 7 Biscupova Street and the actual flat is on the corner of the second floor.

The Moravec flat in Biscupova Street.
The actual flat is on the second floor on the corner of the building

On the corner of the Faculty of Law building of Charles University, very close to a bridge in Prague called Checkuv Most, is a plaque which commemorates the people who were killed by the SS on 5th May 1945. During the occupation, this Law faculty had been taken over by the SS and was used as a barracks. The people killed here were shot and thrown off the bridge in to the Vlatava River. These were patriots who had tried to force the Germans out of their City at the end of the war. To reach this, it is just a short walk from Old Town Square. It's at the far end of a street called Paris Street. Gentlemen beware though, this street is home to all the designer shops featuring brand names like Cartier, Louis Vitton, Hermes and Burberry!

Today

After they were hanged, Frank, Curda and Daluege were supposedly buried in an unmarked grave in the Dablice cemetery in Prague. Sadly, new evidence is coming to light that the remains of the parachutists may have been placed in the very same unmarked grave. If this can be proved, from the evidence available, then this is indeed one of the final tragedies of this whole time. I would urge the authorities to fully investigate this, if it is scientifically possible. There is a new monument placed here, which has an inscription on, which roughly translates as *In this place were, during the Nazi occupation, graves for bodies of patriots who lost their lives for freedom and democracy in Czechoslovakia. There were also bodies of heroic parachutists who on 27/5/1942 attacked and killed Reich Protector Reinhard Heydrich* . There is also a large memorial to the victims of Communism, and many of their graves lie here.

The church of St Cyril and St Methodius (during the German occupation the church was called Charles Borromeo) now stands as a permanent reminder to the "Victims of the Heydrich Terror and Place of Reconciliation". The crypt is now a museum and visitor centre. It is a 'must-see' part of any trip to Prague. Every year on 18th June a Memorial Parade and Service is held here to remember the brave people involved who gave their lives at the Church. On the outside is the plaque featuring a cleric and a parachutist. People often stop by and lay flowers there at the ventilator shaft entrance (which is still surrounded by bullet holes, as is the upstairs part of the church.) On the pavement outside there is the year of 1942 etched into the paving slabs. Near to the church of St Cyril, a new "pub" has opened called the Parachutists and it's a place to have lunch and look at some of the photographs on the wall that are dedicated to these brave people.

There are plaques on the walls of many of the safe houses used by the parachutists. Sadly for people who don't speak other languages, the plaques are only in Czech. Even then they don't clearly point the visitor to which actual location was the place used but only to the nearest big building.

The Prague Military Museum had a magnificent exhibition in 2002 called Assassination. Many items were on display, including even the clothing used by the parachutists when they were hiding in the church. They had a car on display that was claimed to be the actual car Heydrich was attacked in. Whether it was the actual car or not opened up much debate amongst historians and researchers. In his brilliant book *"Enigma"*, writer Max Williams made a very creditable argument to say that it wasn't the correct car, pointing out certain discrepancies such as a different shaped windscreen and rear bumper. He even went as far as to claim that, while it was generally thought that Heydrich's car registration number that day was SS3, he was, in fact, travelling in a car registered as SS4. Indeed, in his report written after the event, the Gestapo investigator Heinz von Pannwitz wrote that the car was SS4. It's possible that the car in the exhibition was one of Heydrich's "official" cars but I don't believe it's the actual car he was attacked in. I believe, from what a number of sources have told me that the actual car is now in private hands in Scandinavia. This marvellous exhibition is in Bratislava at the time of writing, with plans for it to go to Halle and then Vienna. In 2002, to coincide with this exhibition, the seven soldiers who hid in the church were posthumously promoted.

Lidice is now a very poignant memorial site, with a museum, visitor centre, and a number of other memorials for the visitor to learn from. There is a statue of the children at Lidice that really has to be seen to be believed. It is called *"The Memorial to the Child Victims of War"* and was sculptured by a lady called Marie Uchytilova, who sadly spent years creating it but didn't live to see the finished product in bronze. Altogether the statue shows 82 children (42 girls and 40 boys). Of 105 children who were taken from Lidice, only 17 survived the war. Most of the unfortunate children were gassed in the back of a specially modified van at the concentration camp in Chelmno, 82 in fact that are signified in the memorial sculpture.

Likewise, Lezaky has memorials now where the houses in the tiny hamlet once stood. This small hamlet was razed to the ground on 24th June 1942. The day I visited, the place was silent apart from the sound of birds singing and the small river running to a lake. It was a peaceful place. The small visitor centre at Lezaky is open from 1st May until September 30th. It is a long drive from Prague, maybe up to 2 hours depending on traffic.

The site at Pardubice where the people from Lezaky, and others totalling 194 people, were executed between June 3rd and July 9th 1942 (people who were supposed to have had something to do with helping to hide the illegal radio transmitter in the local quarry, or helping parachutists), is now marked with a memorial featuring three stakes to symbolise the stakes in the ground to which the Nazis tied their victims. The victims were shot by members of the Nazi Police Regiment who were based here. The place was part of the Pardubice Chateau. The chateau, however, has long since gone. Now it is called the Memorial Zamacek, which translates as, 'small chateau memorial'. During the war, this place was used as a camp for German cavalry units, police members, and a shooting range for the SS.

The hotel in Pardubice where Josef Valcik had been working as a waiter before being forced to go on the run was demolished in the early 1970's. The Hotel Veselka, as it was called, was demolished as it was in the way of a new road system being built in Pardubice. The owner of the hotel who employed Valcik was a man by the name of Erna Kostal. When Mr Kostal started working for the Resistance he had the foresight to file for a divorce. This saved his family when he was arrested by the Gestapo. Erna Kostal was executed at the Memorial Zamacek. (I am indebted to Mike Janacek, publisher of the Canadian magazine KL, for the information about the hotel)

At Nehvizdy, where the parachutists landed, the Mayor and the towns people are proud of their association. They are keen to talk about it and help in any way they can. I have only ever had a warm welcome and co-operation every time I've been there.

Though the caves where Jan and Josef hid at Nehvizdy are long gone, along with most traces of the quarry, and just about everything else connected to the landing, in 1989 a memorial featuring the names of Jan Kubis and Josef Gabcik, was placed outside the small town hall. The church that gave some assistance to the men is also still there.

The actual bend at Holesovice, the scene of the attack, was altered quite considerably to accommodate a new road system. The bend was made less severe. It is, however, quite easy to find. It is north of Prague and it is still recognisable from the surrounding buildings which have largely stayed unchanged. A comparison between photographs taken at the time and those taken now will easily show the vicinity. The exact place of the attack is just to the right now, on the main road.

The butcher's shop that Josef ran into, in order to try and escape from the chauffeur, is also easy to find. It's no longer a shop and the doorway is gone but, again using comparison photographs, it is easy to see. The actual room that was once the shop now contains all boiler room equipment for the nearby building.

A superb magazine that any researcher should see, and like me, take with them to Prague, is called After the Battle. This brilliant magazine (number 24) has many now-and-then type photographs of Operation Anthropoid, albeit that the memorial at Pardubice is wrongly labelled as being in Lezaky.

The streets near the actual attack site are now named after Gabcik, Kubis, and Valcik. There is talk of a memorial plaque or monument quite rightly being placed in the vicinity of the action. At the time of writing it has not been done, although a small unofficial plaque was placed on a wall nearby. But, thankfully, the authorities have started a competition now for people to submit designs for a new monument, so clearly this is going to be done. Indeed in 2008, a stone was placed in the area as a foundation stone for the monument, and judging by the large size of this, the monument is going to be very impressive!

At the former Gestapo headquarters in Petschek Palace, only a couple of blocks away from Wenceslas Square, there is a plaque on the corner of the building, signifying its sinister history and urging the people to *"be aware"*. For the serious researcher, there is the superb museum inside the basement. Petschek Palace is now home to government trade offices.

In Prague's Pankrac Prison, there is a very sad museum, showing where many people lost their lives at the hands of the Nazis. Included here is the guillotine used by them, which was recovered from the river after the war. (The Germans had thrown it in the river in an attempt to get rid of evidence at the end of the war) The museum is inside the prison grounds and so is not easily accessible.

In Jan Kubis's home village, Dolni Vilemovice in Moravia, about 100 miles south of Prague, there is no plaque on the wall of the house he was born in. I found this quite sad. There is also the house Jan grew up in, again with no plaque. He was born in number 71 and grew up from about the age of 6 in number 79 Dolni Vilemovice. In the centre of his small hamlet there is an old memorial and on this a plaque has been placed commemorating Jan Kubis and members of his family who lost their lives because of Anthropoid. In Dolni Vilemovice Town Hall they have done their local soldier proud. An exhibition is permanently open to Jan Kubis, with photographs, charts and even supposedly part of his recovered parachute. On the outside wall there is a plaque dedicated to the *Memory of National Hero Jan Kubis*. Since 2003 the village has an annual fun-run which is called the Jan Kubis Memorial Run. At the end of the village, the brickworks than Jan used to work in, is now a wood business. The family of Jan Kubis told me that the idea of a statue of Jan was projected after the war but they never heard any more about it.

There are still members of his extended family living in this small village, though sadly, a step-nephew of Jan, Jiri Dusik, died in 2008. I was able to meet Jiri again shortly before he became ill. (I had met him previously when I took Lorna Ellison to Prague) He explained to me how he was arrested and sent to Terezin concentration camp shortly after Anthropoid, even though he was only 1 year old at the time!

The Kubis family, who were so kind and hospitable to me during my visit, told me about the time the Gestapo arrived in the village. They said many German soldiers and Gestapo arrived and took people away in groups. The first group was anyone in the village with the name Kubis. They were taken to Mauthausen concentration camp. Then just over a week later, they returned and took away a second group, which included 1 year old Jiri Dusik. This group were taken to

Terezin. At one time, it was believed that the village of Dolni Vilemovice was to suffer a similar fate to Lidice. It is said, however, that the village Mayor was friendly with some German officials and the village was spared.

The family were so proud to show me the medals and citations Jan had received. They also proudly showed me his personal items returned to the family after the war, most of which fitted in to a small cigarette tin. But Jan's beloved photograph album also survived. I saw Jan's last letter, written to his brother, in which Jan writes that he would like to know if his father is proud that he represents the family, and the village, in the underground war. He also writes about how friendly the Ellison family had been to him, and that he considers them his second family. It is signed *Your Janek Kubis*.

The family told me that Jan's brother Jaroslav was in regular contact with Jan, even after the attack on Heydrich. They believe that Jaroslav visited Jan in Prague and came back with Jan's gun and some documents which he threw away in a river to get rid of evidence.

In nearby Trebice, there is a street named after Jan Kubis and, until recently, there was a school named after him at the end of the street.

Not far from here in Moravia, there is a small village called Resice. It was here that Adolf Opalka lived. When Opalka parachuted back, he hid in his aunts' house in Resice, which now bears a plaque to his memory. It's said that whilst he was hiding here, in order to avoid detection, he even wore ladies clothing whenever he so much as went out into the garden. There is a monument in the village square to Adolf Opalka and the local town hall bears his name. Josef Valcik was born in Smolina, Valasske Klobouky in the east of what is now the Czech Republic. There is a memorial to him there. Members of his family were also executed in Mauthausen

In Slovakia, there are a couple of monuments to Josef Gabcik. On the side of his former home, there is a plaque which roughly translates to read *"In this house on 8 April 1912, Captain Josef Gabcik was born. He was a participant in the assassination of R.Heydrich in Prague 27 May 1942. He was killed by the German Gestapo. Honour his memory!"* The house is in the small hamlet of Poluvsie, about 12 km from Zilina, near the train station. Still living in the house is a member of Josefs family, a lady called Katarina Tomcikova . Her grandfather was Alexandra, Josef's brother. Katarina is proud of her relative Josef and was more than happy to show me around and discuss Josef. I am also pleased to say that after a gap of some years, I was able to put relatives of the Kubis and Gabcik families back in contact with each other.

In Zilina itself there is a big statue of Josef which is fantastic. The statue which was unveiled on 24th May 2002 was designed and made by Stefan Pelikan, with the bust of Josef being made in bronze and weighing 320 kilogram's. The surround of the statue is made from a marble composite, with the inscription roughly translated as *"The leader of the airborne unit Anthropoid and participator in the Assassination of Reinhard Heydrich. To our hero for his activity in the fight for freedom. In memory of Josefs 90th birthday and 60th anniversary of his death. With thanks of the citizens of Zilina"*. The statue is lit up at night and is located outside the main gate of the Slovak Army's Special Operations Regiment HQ. Inside the barracks there is a memorial room with another smaller statue of Josef together with display boards featuring Josef Gabcik and Anthropoid.

In 1995 the Slovak Army's 5th Special Operations Regiment, was given the honorary title of the Zilina Regiment of Josef Gabcik. Every year there is an army competition in Josef's name. There is also a Josef Gabcik annual fun run from Josef's house to the Regiments barracks.

In Britain, there were obviously a number of places connected to Operation Anthropoid but, sadly, there is not a great deal to see any more. At Cholmondoley Castle in Cheshire, where the Czechoslovak Brigade was first properly stationed, there is a memorial stone enclosed by a small railing, in the castle grounds. This stone is not to Anthropoid but rather it commemorates all the Czechoslovak soldiers based there.

At Chester Cathedral there is a wall-mounted plaque to all the Czechoslovak soldiers and airmen who served.

The Czechoslovak soldiers, including the men of Anthropoid, were moved to the area around Leamington Spa. In the town's Jephson gardens there is one of my favourite memorials, a superb fountain in the shape of a parachute. The top of the fountain holds the names of the seven parachutists who died in Prague's St Cyril's Church. On the floor nearby, there is a plaque explaining Operation Anthropoid.

3-8 Porchester Gate on London's Bayswater Road was used as the Headquarters of Czechoslovak Military Intelligence and, where I believe, many of the decisions connected with Anthropoid were taken. At the back of this building, in the service courtyard, there is a red-brick wall. Against this wall, final photographs of every parachutist were taken, before they were flown out for their various missions. The wall is unchanged. Every attempt to contact the owners of this luxury block of flats, to put a plaque on the wall, has gone unanswered.

At Aston House, near Stevenage, where Jan and Josef practised attacking on a moving car, there is very little to see. Most of the grounds have now become part of a golf course.

At Everton village hall in Bedfordshire there is a memorial plaque and an explanation about Anthropoid and its cost in lives. There is nothing left of the building which housed the radio station at Woldingham. The site was levelled and a new bungalow built in its place. This radio station provided vital contact with the Resistance in the Protectorate, during the time of Anthropoid.

There are plans, I believe, to put a memorial of a parachute in the village of Arisaig in Scotland, where some of the training for Anthropoid took place. The Anthropoid men were here for some intensive training given by 2 specialists called Sykes and Bush.

In Berlin, there isn't a great deal left to see. Much of Berlin was bombed and damaged, particularly towards the end of the war, and has since been rebuilt. However, Berlin is becoming more open to its past and there are now guide maps and even signposts for the history visitor to use, especially around the area that is called Wilhelmstrasse, which was the area of many of the main Nazi buildings. Heydrich's main Gestapo office in Prinz Albrecht Street has gone, although there is a new exhibition on the site called "Topography of Terror".

The house in Wannsee near Berlin, where the infamous Conference chaired by Heydrich, took place in January 1942, is well worth a visit. The staff are very co-operative, and most of the display boards are in English. The Conference room itself is very insignificant and it's hard to believe that it was in this room, the former dining room of the Villa, that the *"final solution to the Jewish problem"* was largely devised. The grounds of the villa, on the edge of the lake, are so peaceful. It is so easy to understand why this place was popular with high-ranking Nazis, and the juxtaposition of what took place here is hard to imagine.

The Plotzensee Prison is an important part of the story of the Third Reich. Although it is still a working prison, the Memorial to the many people who lost their lives here, including Czech Resistance fighters and also many of the people involved in the 1944 Hitler bomb plot, is accessible to the public. The Memorial is based at the former execution chamber of the prison.

On or around Fehmarn Island, (a small island in Northern Germany), there are a number of places associated with the life of Reinhard Heydrich, including his wife's burial place at St Jurgen cemetery in Burg auf Fehmarn. The gravestone still has her former married name of Heydrich inscribed. Also inscribed is her name when she remarried a Finnish man by the surname of Manninen. The grave is in the family plot of von Osten and is located very near to the chapel. The guest house which Lina Heydrich ran after the war has now been replaced by a large hotel called the Hotel Intersol which is located on the Burgtiefe, the promenade of Burg. One of Heydrich's daughters runs a successful and upmarket fashion shop near here.

Just off the island there is the house Lina was living in with her parents at the time she met her future husband and where he visited her parents for the first time. This is in a small village called Lutjendorfe. The house, which was the old schoolhouse, is now partly a youth hostel. In the next village, which is called Grossenbrode, the church of St Katherine's is easily found. This is the church where the Heydrichs were married, with the groom wearing top hat and tails! The church is unusual as part of it dates back hundreds of years and is in part wooden. In the grounds of the church there are a number of soldiers' graves from World War 2, including a grave that contains thirty Russian prisoners.

Heydrich's huge 6 foot 7 inches tall chauffer, Johannes Klein lived out the war. He recovered from the gunshot wounds inflicted outside the butcher's shop but was said to walk with a pronounced limp. He lived near Düsseldorf where for a number of years he made his living selling food ingredients.

At the time of the attack, Heydrich was wearing his grey officer's tunic, with a few awards on it. He was not wearing all of his medals or ribbons, as he only wore all these on special state occasions. On the tunic's left hand side, Heydrich was wearing, above his top pocket, the Luftwaffe Long Range Day Fighters Clasp. This was awarded for a pilot making 60 flights (Heydrich was awarded this medal both in bronze and silver). Below his top left pocket was his Golden Party Badge, his Iron Cross first class, which he received for Luftwaffe service on the eastern front and, below that, a cloth version of his Combined Pilot and Observers Badge in Gold and Diamonds. This was apparently awarded personally by Hermann Goering, who was in charge of the Luftwaffe. He also wore in his button-hole the red ribbon of his Iron Cross second class which he had been awarded for Luftwaffe service on the western front. He wore plain grey trousers with no stripe down the outsides, a white shirt, white shorts and a white vest. The clothes have survived and are in a private collection within Europe. I am privileged to be one of the few people to have seen and examined them after I spent many years trying to track them. Eventually this *"Holy Grail"* of the Anthropoid story was in my hands, from a very unusual source but one that I gave my word to not reveal. The outer officer's tunic, made by a Berlin company called Herman Frank (no connection to Karl Hermann Frank), shows just a small puncture tear slightly to the left of centre, midway up the back. I was surprised how small the hole in the coat was. It is lacerated a bit, but not much. The shirt is more lacerated and contains bloodstains, as does the vest, and the top of the trousers and shorts.

Some theories say that Heydrich was wearing a bullet-proof vest on the day he was attacked. My research can't confirm or deny this although Heider Heydrich categorically denied he wore one. But even if he was, it clearly didn't save him from being injured in the back.

After the assassination, the Germans introduced a series of postage stamps bearing Heydrich's death mask. These are quite collectable and are often available on eBay or from dealers.

For the collector, there are also some quirky things available to buy, such as plastic model dolls of Heydrich, metal figures of Heydrich and even metal figures of the car and figures of the main players at the scene of the attack issued by a company called King and Country.

In 1992 in the Czech Republic, a first-day postage stamp was issued for the 50th anniversary of Anthropoid featuring Gabcik and Kubis.

For the serious collector, a Heydrich signature is most sought-after and expensive to purchase. A document with Heydrich's original signature will cost several thousands of pounds, depending on the quality, date and importance of the document. Most documents bearing his signature have just the word "Heydrich" signed on them. This was quite a common way for high-ranking Nazis to sign their name as it signified an imperialistic standing. There are occasionally other Heydrich-related items of interest in private hands which see the light of day, like the fencing statue photographed in this book. This was presented by his fencing comrades to Heydrich in 1936, around the time of a major fencing competition. It has the inscription *"For party member and Major General Reinhard Heydrich, in true comradeship, from your fencing friend 2nd Lieutenant SS Kretschmann, and the fencing comrades"*. Someone has this in a private collection.

After the war, Lina Heydrich fought the authorities for a number of years and eventually won the right to be awarded a pension as the widow of a General killed in action.

She also wrote her biography which she called *'Living with a War Criminal'* but it was only printed in German. Though there are unconfirmed reports of Heydrich having other offspring, it is a fact that he had four children with Lina. The eldest boy, Klaus, was killed twelve months after his father, when he was knocked down by a bus, whilst riding his bicycle outside the gates of the family home in Prague. The other three surviving children are still alive at the time of writing this book, Heider the son, and two daughters Silke and Marte. I have met Heydrich's daughter Marte, who wasn't born until after her father's death, on two occasions. By checking names against telephone and other records, as well as visiting Fehmarn Island, I was able to eventually find her. Lina Heydrich was pregnant with Marte at the time of the assassination and, as a consequence, was unable to travel to Berlin for her husband's funeral. Marte is a very stylish and smart lady, as one may expect of someone running a swish, upmarket ladies fashion boutique. If someone told me that she and her father were twins I would believe them. Marte looks remarkably like him. The first time I met her she was wearing a black trouser suit and this, coupled with her blonde hair and identical looks, made me stop in my tracks! It could have been her father! She was polite to me but refused any of my attempts to talk about her father. At first she denied being Marte, then, when she realised I knew quite a lot of information about her life, she said she didn't speak English. The next day she did! The same applies to her son, also called Reinhard, who wouldn't talk about his grandfather, when I contacted him on the telephone. Faced with any requests to talk about Reinhard Heydrich, the family always seem to refer to the surviving son Heider Heydrich who lives near Munich. This is clearly a rehearsed and worked out ploy to deflect any possible unwelcome media intrusion into their private lives, which is fair enough, and understandable.

I will always be grateful to Heider for agreeing to talk to me. Once I had gained his trust he never refused to answer my questions and so, due to him, the story of Operation Anthropoid became much clearer to me. I now count him as a friend and we remain in regular contact with each other.

Der Reichsminister des Innern

Pol. S I A 2 a Nr. 819/41

Bitte in der Antwort vorstehendes Geschäftszeichen und Datum
anzugeben.

Berlin SW 11, den ___20. März___ 19~~35~~ 42
Prinz-Albrecht-Straße 8
Fernsprecher: 12 00 40

An den

Regierungsoberinspektor

Herrn Wilhelm L u d w i g

im H a u s e .

Durch die anliegende Urkunde habe ich Sie zum
Regierungsamtmann ernannt. Gleichzeitig übertrage
ich Ihnen mit Wirkung vom 1. Februar 1942 ab eine
freie Planstelle für Regierungsamtmänner der Besol-
dungsgruppe A 3 b bei dem Reichssicherheitshauptamt
(Hauptamt Sicherheitspolizei) in Berlin.

Wegen Berechnung und Anweisung der erhöhten Be-
züge wird das Referat II C 4 des Reichssicherheits-
hauptamtes das Weitere veranlassen.

Im Auftrage

[signature]

An example of a Heydrich signature. This one on a letter to Mr Wilhelm Ludwig explains about a promotion and also informs Mr Ludwig that his earnings will be raised!

Further Reading

The Czech Connection
Neil Rees 2005 Czechoslovak
Government-in-Exile Research Society

Heydrich. The Face of Evil
Mario R Dederichs 2006 Greenhill Books

Reinhard Heydrich. The Biography
Volume 1 Road To War
Max Williams 2001 Ulric Publishing

Reinhard Heydrich. The Biography
Volume 2 Enigma
Max Williams 2003 Ulric Publishing

Prague in the shadow of the Swastika
Callum MacDonald and Jan Kaplan 1995
Quartet Books Ltd

Assassination
Czech Republic Ministry of Defence
2002

Lidice. The Story of a Czech Village
Eduard Stehlik 2004 Lidice Memorial

Reinhard Heydrich. Assassination
Ray R. Cowdrey 1994 USM Incorporated

Heydrich The Pursuit of Total Power
Gunther Deschner 1981 Orbis Publishing
Ltd

After the Battle Magazine number 24
1979 Battle of Britain Prints International
Ltd

Leamingtons Czech Patriots
Alan Griffin 2004 Feldon Books

National Cleansing
Benjamin Frommer 2005 Cambridge
University Press

Heydrich Henchman of Death
Charles Whiting 1999 Leo Cooper

The Life and Times of Reinhard Heydrich
G.S. Graber 1980 David McKay
Company Inc.

Target Heydrich
Miroslav Ivanov 1972 Macmillan
Publishing Co., Inc

Seven Men at Daybreak
Alan Burgess 1960 Evans Brothers Ltd

The Czechs under Nazi Rule
Vojtech Mastny 1971 Columbia
University Press

The Czech Lands 1918-1994
Jiri Pokorny 1994 Prah-Martin Vopenka

With Blood and With Iron
J.B. Hutak 1957 Robert Hale Limited

The Killing of SS Obergruppenfuhrer
Reinhard Heydrich
Callum MacDonald 1989 Collier Books

The Villa, The Lake, The Meeting
Mark Roseman 2002 Penguin Books

Akce Atentat (Czech language only)
Jaroslav Cvancara 1991 Magnet Press

Gestapo Instrument of Tyranny
Edward Crankshaw 1956 Greenhill Books

History of the SS
G.S. Graber 1978 Robert Hale Limited

An Illustrated History of the Gestapo
Rupert Butler 1992 BCA